The Most 7 Expensive Mistakes Salon Owners Make...

"and how to solve them virtually overnight."

Simon Lotinga

The 7 Most Expensive Mistakes Salon Owners Make...
and how to solve them virtually overnight

First published in Great Britain in 2010
by SLC Publishing

www.simonlotingaconsulting.com
01205 366599

ISBN 978-1-907308-05-5

Set by The Book Refinery Ltd

Printed in Great Britain by the MPG Books Group,
Bodmin and King's Lynn

This publication is designed to provide accurate and authoritative information for the owners of Hairdressing Salons. It is sold under the express understanding any decisions or actions you take as a result of reading this book must be based on your commercial judgement and will be at your sole risk. The author will not be held responsible for the consequences of any actions and/or decisions taken as a result of any information given or recommendations made.

If legal, tax, accounting or other expert assistance is required you should seek the services of a competent professional.

Dedication

If you've ever lived with someone who's writing a book you'll know how 'distracted' they can become.

I'd like to dedicate this book to my wife Sue and tell her, now it's finished she can have her husband back!

Contents

Preface: A Tale of Two Frogs 7

Introduction: A Book For Salon Owners... 11

Expensive Mistake Number 1
Avoiding The Fight You HAVE to Win... 23

Expensive Mistake Number 2
Thinking It's 'OK' to be The Weakest Link... 37

Expensive Mistake Number 3
Putting up With 'Hyacinth'... 49

Expensive Mistake Number 4
Employing The Wrong People... 59

Expensive Mistake Number 5
Running a 'JOKE' Business... 73

Expensive Mistake Number 6
Giving The Gossips The Chance to... 83

Expensive Mistake Number 7
Missing 'The 'X' Factor'... 105

Finally: What's Next For You... 111

Preface
The Tale of Two Frogs.

Once upon a time a group of frogs lived in a pond on a farm. They were normal frogs in every way, except one of them, called Fred, was profoundly deaf.

One day Fred and his mate Ginger decided to go for a hop to see what was new. They were having a great time exploring and after a while found themselves down by the cow shed which was full of exciting things for curious frogs to explore. You know the sort of thing I mean. Lots of shade, some damp corners to dig around in and nice mouldy smells as well.

When they'd had enough and were about to leave, Ginger discovered the farmer had left a bucket of fresh milk by the door.

Now I don't know if you know this, but most frogs 'love' milk and Ginger and Fred were no exception. Finding a whole bucket of it was just too much of a temptation for them so they hopped in and had a drink.

They were in heaven and truth be told, they probably drank a little bit more than they should; but we've all done that at some point in our lives, haven't we!

Anyway, after they'd had enough and decided it was time to go, they began to realise they had a problem. They were trapped in the bucket and couldn't get out.

They'd drunk so much milk that the level had dropped quite a long way and the rim of the bucket was now too high for them to reach!

With nothing to leap from, or grab on to, all they could do was keep swimming round looking for a means to escape. They also tried croaking really loudly for help and sure enough it wasn't long before the other frogs heard the noise and came to see what the problem was.

They hopped up and looked down into the bucket, saw Fred and Ginger swimming round desperately trying to find a way out of their predicament and after a lot of discussion... decided there was nothing they could do.

In fact, they decided, the situation was so hopeless that a few of the frogs started to get cross with the pair for managing to get themselves into such a mess in the first place.

Gradually the others picked up on the mood of anger and hysteria and before long they were all jumping up and down, waving their arms about, and shouting abuse at the stricken frogs!

They said things like:

- *"You're a couple of stupid ****s for getting into this mess."*
- *"Why didn't you think more carefully about what might happen before you dived in there."*
- *"Don't blame us for not being able to get you out, it's entirely your fault and there's nothing we can do!"*

Ginger heard all this criticism, judgement and negativity. He really took it to heart. After a while his efforts to get out became feeble. Eventually, he gave up trying, sank to the bottom and drowned.

Poor ginger.

But Fred; well Fred was deaf wasn't he! He didn't know that the situation was **'hopeless'** because he couldn't hear what the other frogs were saying.

He thought that all their waving and jumping around was actually encouragement ... so he didn't give up.

He tried and tried and do you know what happened?

Eventually all his flapping, thrashing and churning started to turn the milk into butter. He kept persevering and eventually it got so thick he was able to leap out!

Fred hopped away a sadder, wiser frog and he went on to live a long and productive life; obviously, poor old Ginger didn't!

That's the end of our simple tale, but what do you think's the moral of the story?

Well, there are several if you look and I'll let you decide which one means the most to you.

All I know; is when it comes to running my salon:

- I choose to be the frog who can't hear the narrow minded defeatists and doom mongers.
- I choose to be the frog who believes anything is possible.
- I choose to be the frog who takes support and encouragement from wherever I can find it.
- I choose to be the frog who doesn't give up.
- I choose to be like Fred

You have a choice too and it's an important one because you're about to read this book. It's a book that can change your salon and change your life.

If you want proof, just look at the beginning of every chapter and you'll find a testimonial from a salon owner who's already read the book and used the ideas tools and principles inside it.

You'll see they **know** it works; you'll see they want you to know it works too ... but unless you take the lessons from the tale of Fred and Ginger to heart and make a conscious choice to be like Fred you won't get the best from it.

So:

- If you want the results this book promises.
- If you want a salon that makes more profit for you, more easily.
- If you want a team that works hard and is easy to manage.
- If you want, more choice, more flexibility and more freedom in your life;
- Choose to be like Fred as well.

Enjoy the book!

"A Book for Hairdressing Salon Owners!"

As you read this book you'll notice there's very little mention of hairdressing itself, because it's not that sort of book. So I'd better explain what sort of book it is! It's a book for salon owners who want their salon to be more successful, but haven't discovered the secret to making it happen.... **YET!**

If that describes you, then read on, I promise you'll love it!

By the way, it's not a long book, and it isn't full of business jargon either; so you'll discover you can read it easily in an hour or two. Don't let the fact that it's not a long book fool you, because it's jam packed full of the sort advice that will make a real difference - **if you use it!**

I've written it for you, because I was in the same situation once, with a salon that was driving me **'nuts'** and none of the standard solutions and typical industry advice I could get my hands on helped me very much.

In the end I went on a journey outside the hairdressing industry and found many interesting tools and concepts, which I refined, adapted and applied to my salon and it got better, **much** better!

I'll share some of the story with you as we go along, but for now I want to tell you how the journey started; and it started with a feeling.

I wonder if you know the one I mean?

It's that feeling you get when you realise that something obvious has been stuck right under your nose trying to get your **ATTENTION** for a very long time, but you just don't notice, then suddenly...

BANG! you do!

Not only do you feel **'IT'** and see **'IT'** you also realise just how obvious **'IT'** has always been, if only you'd been looking.

Well.

That's exactly how I felt when it suddenly dawned on me I'd discovered the reason why so many salon owners, *including me before I got **'IT'***, have to struggle so hard to make our salons the stress free, profitable businesses they ought to be. Now I promise I'll tell you what I realised in just a moment, but before I do, there's something else we need to be aware of.

I want you to imagine for a moment you're a fly.

That's right, a fly!

And imagine you're buzzing round a room that's full of salon owners who are all talking to each other. Imagine they're talking about their salons; do you think, you'd get the impression from listening to them, they were all doing OK?

It's pretty likely isn't it!

Very few of us are happy to admit that things aren't going as well as we'd want, but sadly this is often an illusion. The reality can be rather different. How do I know? Because, after I'd done such a good job of sorting my own salon out, I was swamped with questions from other salon owners wanting to know how I did it. To help them I created my '**S**alon **O**wner **S**urvival' system which for obvious reasons has become affectionately known as the ***"SOS"** system*!

I've now had the pleasure of working with thousands of salon owners and run many ***"SOS"*** based courses and on nearly every course the same thing happens. There comes a point when a salon owner feels confident enough to start talking about the problems they're having: with their staff, with their bank balance, with the taxman, with their partner, or whatever issue it is that's bothering them.

When they do, other salon owners say: "I know how you feel, **I thought it was only me who had problems like that!"**

This is absolutely true.

I've seen it happen time after time. So it's OK to be **'honest'** about your problems while you're reading this book because you're not alone. Most salon owners get it wrong before they get it right. As I've already mentioned, I certainly did, in fact I got it **spectacularly** wrong.

I was doing what **<u>seemed</u>** to be all the right things and yet I managed to create:

- A business that made me feel trapped;
- A business I didn't enjoy;
- A business that gave me constant staff problems, and lots of worry about how I was going to pay my bills.

When I started to understand and implement everything you'll read about in this book, my salon changed and in fact it **<u>tripled</u>** in size over the next 5 years.

And that's not all. As well as seeing growth, I also saw staff problems melting away as they developed into a stable happy team who now produce good profits, cause me very few problems and only need me to do what I enjoy doing, **on a <u>very</u> part time basis.**

Now if you're still in the getting it wrong phase, don't worry, we've agreed it's not surprising and it does happen to nearly everyone. The good news is you just have to **<u>believe</u>** there's an alternative, **<u>believe</u>** you can do something about it, and everything will start to change.

That's what this book is for.

To show you how to move from the stressed out reality of getting it wrong, to the feeling of pride, profit and satisfaction you get, when you get it **RIGHT.**

But before we get into the meat of the book, I promised to let you in on the secret of **'IT'**, didn't I! **'IT'** is actually quite simple. **'IT'** is the fact that we often end up with problems, simply because we start a business for the **wrong** reason.

When I say the wrong reason, I don't mean we don't **'have'** a good reason, because most of them are **very** good reasons and most of them motivate us very powerfully - **in the beginning.** But it's the **in the beginning** bit where the problem lies.

Let me explain. Motivation is a word used to describe something that gets you to take action.

It can be broken down into 2 very simple categories:

1. **Towards'** motivation.
2. **Away'** motivation.

This means as human beings we're either attracted to move **towards** something we want; like the warm fuzzy feelings we get when we see something attractive or buy something nice. Or we find ourselves repelled and move **away** from something we don't want; like negative feelings, pain, or the fear of losing something we love or value! Does that make sense?

So which type of motivation got **you** to make the decision to become the owner of a hairdressing business? Let's look at the most common reasons I'm given when I've asked salon owners this question, and see if any match your own experience:

- You may have worked for a salon owner who wanted to sell up, get out or retire and they needed someone to take the business over, so it could carry on. Because you're already there working as an employee; and because you **'know'** the business, you decide its **'safe'** to buy it.

- Or you may have been in the same situation as above, with an owner who wants to move on. Taking on a salon was **not** something you ever considered or really wanted, but now you feel under pressure to do it. Why? Because if you don't, everyone including **you** will need to find new jobs, **so you buy the business.**

- Or you may have been a successful stylist who got to the point where you felt worth more than any boss was prepared *(or could afford)* to pay you, so you leave and open your own salon, **so you can take control of what you earn.**

- Or you may have been a successful stylist who got fed up with feeling de-motivated, and being taken for granted. Fed up with working in a bitchy atmosphere and being managed badly. Finally it gets so bad you decide to start your own salon, **where you promise yourself things will be different.**

- Or you may have had a client, a parent or a friend with money who kept telling you, **'you can do it'** and was prepared to put some or all the money up. Because of their **'belief'** in you and the fact that the money's available, **you decide to start your own salon.**

There are plenty of other reasons we could talk about. These are the most common, and they're all **very** good, **very** normal, **very** understandable reasons, that get us to take action and either buy an existing business or start one from scratch.

So what's the problem?

Try thinking about it this way; all the reasons we've just talked about are 'away' motivation reasons. Why? In each case it's because the trigger for starting or buying a salon was **'outside'** of you. This means it's highly likely you started your salon because **someone else** decided to either:

- Move on;
- Guilt trip you into doing it;
- Not value you enough;
- Value you more than you do yourself;
- Or simply behave badly towards you.

Put that way it's a bit of an eye opener, isn't it!

So what's the problem with buying or starting a salon using 'away' motivation? Well, it's all a question of energy and focus.

'Away' motivation is good for making things happen. It's good for beginnings, but the problem with it is simple: **it's effects don't last.** 'Away' motivation gives us the reason to get started; but after the initial excitement and adrenaline rush of getting everything organised and opening our doors to paying clients, the **'what next'** question needs answering. And we do answer it: **sort of!**

Why only sort of?

Because in the early days of growing our business, we're still trying to get on top everything; so 'what next' normally boils down to getting more established, which means getting:

- **More** clients;
- **More** staff;
- **More** turnover;
- **More** profit.

In fact, simply getting the business to **'the point'** where it feels safe and logical to make some real 'what next' decisions.

Fact: Very few salon owners get to the point where they feel they can make those decisions.

Why not?

Because, typically somewhere between **1** and **7** years after we open, something happens so gradually **we don't even notice!** We lose sight of the point where we feel safe to plan an exciting future and find ourselves stuck in a **'RUT'** instead.

After all:

- Bills have to be paid;

- Staff **'issues'** can't be ignored;
- The tax man won't go away.

So we get stuck in a 'RUT' dealing with all this stuff! A 'RUT' is just ***"A grave with the end kicked out!"*** A grave is a place where we get **'buried'** and in so many salons, the hopes, dreams and wishes of salon owners get buried too.

What do most of us do when life gets a bit too much for us and we want some light relief?

We watch TV of course!

The good news is, if we look carefully there are lots of useful things we can learn while we're watching. Lessons we can use to get out of the 'RUT'. Lessons we can use to create some much needed 'towards' motivation.

Ah... 'towards' motivation, I expect you were wondering when we'd get to that!

'Away' motivation is great for getting us to take short term action, and make powerful changes, but when it comes to long term sustainable growth and a healthy business, it has to be combined with 'towards' motivation for the effects to last.

Think of it this way.

Imagine you're running in a race.

It makes sense to get a fast start, doesn't it, and using 'away' motivation is a great way to make a powerful start. But if a fast start is all you've got, you'll run out of steam **before** you get to the finishing line.

If you want to get over that line, especially if you want to get over it as a winner, you need to add a great big dollop of 'towards' motivation to the mixture to keep you focussed and drive you on.

Now let's take the running a race example a step further. A lot of salon owners are great at starting things, I suppose it's because most of us by nature are pretty creative. **The problem is, because we get bored or distracted easily, we're not so good at finishing them!**

Let's turn this common trait among us to our advantage and enter a **different** type of race.

A RELAY RACE

A relay race is simply a running race that's split into legs with several runners taking part as a team and a baton that's passed from runner to runner. Let's imagine we run the first leg using 'away' motivation to give us the focus, excitement and energy we need. At the point where we are running out of steam we pass the baton on to our next motivating idea, then the next, and so on, till our business crosses the line as a **winner!**

Now the important thing to focus on is what happens at the point where the baton is passed from one runner to the next.

Does it come to a complete stop? **NO!** The second runner starts running **before** the first runner gets to them, so the baton keeps moving as it changes hands.

You've got to do the same with your motivation. You've got to make a start on your next big idea, **before** the previous one's finished.

And if you're not good at finishing things, *a problem many salon owners will admit to*, you must get someone else to finish your previous idea for you, while you make a start on the next one!

If you don't get your motivation passed on safely, it's like dropping the baton during a relay race, because as far as you're concerned it's over, ***you just fell into your 'RUT'!***

Now I understand this important lesson, nearly all I do these days is have a great idea, get it organised and prove it works. Then I delegate it to someone who is **excited** by the opportunity and they carry it on for me. It's a simple concept isn't it, and as I discovered, very easy to do, so why don't more salon owners do it?

I'll explain **'why'** in the next chapter but for now just remember why I wrote this book, ***to give you the tools to get out of the typical salon owners 'RUT'.***

We're going to do it by talking about what we can learn from watching TV! We'll be looking at **7** very popular programmes and each one will teach us a powerful lesson. Each lesson highlights an expensive mistake we can make and by the time we've covered all **7** you're going to be unstoppable!!!

By the way, as we go through the book I describe various clips from the TV programmes I'm talking about. I recommend several great books for you to read, and I also mention some useful websites you could visit.

You'll also hear more about my ***"SOS"*** *system* and you'll be pleased to know I'll be sharing parts of it with you as we go through.

To make it easy for you to find everything, I've put it all in one place at **www.7expensivemistakes.com**

So, if you'd like to actually **see** the TV clips, read more about the books, go to the websites or print copies of the material from my ***"SOS"*** *system* to use in your own salon, you know where to go!

To help you, I'll remind you of the site address at the end of each chapter. So let's get started!

"Read this easy rule book ... and you'll never look back!"

"As someone who was in exactly the same boat as Simon describes in this book it seemed I was stuck in the 'RUT' at a dead end with nowhere to turn ... until I started using the lessons it contains.

At first everything seemed way out of my comfort zone and I wondered how it would ever help, but soon my confidence and motivation returned ... I didn't feel quite so stressed and felt a bit more like ME!

Once I got to that point, I could see changes happening and light at the end of the tunnel ... not only with the business, but with my staff, myself and my personal life! My advice to you is ... read this easy rule book and you'll never look back!"

Julia Suttie, Allure Hair and Beauty

Expensive Mistake Number 1
Avoiding the fight you HAVE to win!

I can remember the first time I ever saw **'Ramsay's Kitchen Nightmares'** as if it was yesterday. Why has it stuck in my mind long after I've forgotten just about everything else? I suppose it's because it hadn't occurred to me until then how similar a salon and a restaurant are.

Once Gordon Ramsay showed me that the **'recipes'** for making them successful were almost identical, it became obvious that the programme was going to be chock full of important lessons I could adapt and use to make my salon better.

Why are they so similar?

- I think it's because the majority of restaurants are small, independent businesses, **just like our salons.**
- The majority of restaurants struggle to make a consistent profit, **just like most salon owners do.**
- The mistakes restaurateurs and salon owners make when it comes to leadership, organisation, people management, money management and marketing seem to be very similar as well. So I suppose when you think about it, it shouldn't be surprising that the fundamental principles that drive successful salons and restaurants **are almost identical.**

All of which means, when someone gives a master class on how to turn round a failing restaurant, every salon owner in the country should have their eyes **glued** to their TV to see what they can learn.

Sadly we haven't got time to go through every episode and analyse every lesson in a book like this. To make it workable I've selected a 10 minute clip that shows very clearly the first expensive mistake I see salon owners making. Don't forget you can see it for yourself at www.7expensivemistakes.com.

At the beginning of the clip we join Gordon saying goodbye as he's leaving a Restaurant in Blackpool after helping them for a week.

We then see him return 8 months later to see how they're getting on, **and it's <u>not</u> good news.**

He's dismayed to discover that within **weeks** of his departure they fell back in to a lot of the bad habits he'd helped them change.

For example:

- They started closing in the evenings again - **to save money.**
- They let some of their staff go - **to save money.**
- They went back to using cheap commercial catering ingredients instead of the fresh **'Home Cooked'** ingredients Gordon introduced them - **to save money.**

I could go on!

Their actions pose a question we all need to consider very carefully. "If business got really tough for you, like it did for the couple in this clip, **would you do what they did?"**

Would you cut back, dumb down and simply try to survive by being cheaper than the competition?

Or would your natural instinct be to fight on because you believe passionately in:

- Yourself;
- Your team;
- Your concept.

Would you use this passion to get over any obstacles in your way so you can go forward, grow and build?

If you decided to cut back, it would be understandable, after all cutting back is easy and a pound saved ... is a pound saved. But, and it's a **BIG BUT,** cutting back can be **very** short sighted because it often leads you into a trap.

Think about it.

What would happen if you kept on cutting and cutting and **cutting?** Taken to its logical conclusion you'd be left with:

- No staff;
- No premises;
- **JUST YOU!!!**

Go to this extreme and your only option will be to rent a chair, or become a freelance hairdresser. Is that what you want? Of course you can make a living like this, but it will **never** be more than that. You'll only ever be paid for the time you put in.

That's it!

If this isn't the sort of existence you want, then you have to look at the alternative - **which is to fight.**

The first thing you have to fight for is your belief in yourself.

Why?

- Because belief comes before confidence: **Your confidence.**
- Confidence comes before action: **Your action.**
- Action comes before success: **Your success.**

Fact: Dig away at any business that's either stagnating or constantly struggling with problems and you'll find an owner who's fighting the 'hidden enemy' ... a poor self image.

The evidence this battle is going on reveals itself in many ways but if you recognise **any** of the following symptoms then you're probably in the middle of a fight with your own hidden enemy.

Do you find:

- Nothing gets done unless you nag?

- It's often easier to do things yourself?
- It's hard to put up prices because you don't want to lose clients or deal with the moans from your staff?
- Your staff room atmosphere is quite bitchy?
- It's hard to confront **'difficult'** people?
- You keep losing staff?
- That your salon struggles to grow?
- You find it hard to trust some of your staff?
- You can be moody or stressed out at work?

If you answered yes to even **one** of these questions, then the signs are you're paying a high price and I strongly believe you have to do something about it! You have to work at improving your self image as a matter of urgency.

When you do, **everything** else we're going to talk about becomes possible. Put off doing it, as many of you will, and you'll find the other ideas I'm going to share with you simply won't work. In other words a positive self image and the high self esteem that go with it are **the** foundation for everything else you want.

We can see this quite clearly in the clip I've described.

Gordon achieved a lot in the week he spent at the restaurant, **but he didn't manage to change the owner's belief in himself and what was possible.** How do we know? Because the minute the pressure was on, the owner went back to his old way of behaving. He'd gone through the process of change with Gordon, but as we can see it was **only** at surface level.

His internal picture or in other words his **'self image'** hadn't changed.

So let me just emphasise the point. **'Your business is always going to be a reflection of YOU'** so if you're going to fight for your business, the first battle you need to win is with **yourself**!

How can a poor self image be so damaging?

Think of it like the **'Windows'** operating software on a computer. When it's working properly, your computer can do fantastic things. When it isn't,

nothing works the way it should and you find yourself wasting time, getting frustrated and going round in circles.

Your self image controls **your** operating software, which is made up of:

- Your emotions;
- Your beliefs;
- Your behaviour patterns.

Your emotions can be positive or negative, and we all live with a mixture of both, but in the same way a computer has a **'safe'** mode to revert to when things go wrong, your subconscious mind has a **'safe'** emotional response to fall back on when you're under pressure!

Let me show you how damaging it is for our **'safe'** emotions to be negative; and we'd better start by looking at a list of the most common negative emotions:

- Anger;
- Fear;
- Guilt;
- Sadness;
- Hurt.

Now let's make these negative emotions come alive.

We all know people who get **'angry'**:

- They blow up for the slightest reason, don't they.

- They're often bullies, aren't they. And we respond to them in different ways depending on the state of our own self image.

- We either choose to confront them, avoid them completely, or walk on eggshells if we **'have'** to deal with them!

We all know people who are ruled by **'fear'**:

- We know they can be indecisive, hard to motivate and absolutely **hate** confrontation.

- They may be frightened of failure or getting things wrong, **so they don't take risks.**

- They may be frightened of success, **so they sabotage anything that starts to go well because they think they don't 'deserve' it.**

- They may be frightened of looking silly, being seen as cocky or standing out from the crowd.

- They may be afraid people won't like them, **so they try to 'please' everyone.**

We all know people who are driven by **'guilt'**:

- No matter what they do, they feel **'guilty'** about not **'doing'** enough, or not being **'good'** enough.

- More often than not their guilt drives them to be impossible to help, or please, or even worse they can be unreasonable perfectionists.

- You know who I mean don't you? No matter **what** you do for them it's never enough, or good enough, is it!

We all know people who are **'sad'**:

- They're glass half empty people who tend to notice and dwell on the negative news and incidents that happen to all of us at different times in our lives.

- Because of their perspective they see setbacks and tragedies as confirmation of their view of the problems and sadness of the world.

We all know people who wallow in **'hurt'**:

- They tend to be life's **'victims'**.

- They focus obsessively on the people and events they feel have damaged them, or robbed them. They use these events to feed and justify their behaviour.

- To them, the reasons for their problems are always outside of them selves; when things go wrong it's **never** their fault, they've always got an excuse!

We all see and know people like these don't we, but what most of us don't realise is how often other people look at **us and see the same sort of behaviour:**

OUCH!

I mentioned earlier that **'limiting beliefs'** hold us back as well and as you'll see in a moment they nearly always go hand in hand with **negative emotions**.

The good news is **beliefs don't have to be limiting,** they can be empowering too.

I'm so passionate about the idea that positive empowering beliefs are a vital tool in helping us get out of the **'RUT'** that I wrote a poem to remind me about it. It's called **'If you think you can'** and it goes like this:

If you think you're beaten, you are
If you believe you can't, you won't try
If you want to win but you're not sure you can
Life will pass you by

If you think you'll lose, you've lost
When you look for the reason you'll find
Success begins with what you believe
It's all in your state of mind

Success in this life isn't won
By the strongest or fastest man
When all's said and done the one who wins
Is the man who believes he can

As you can see from those words I truly **'believe'** our beliefs are the foundation of our results, and a poor self image leads to limiting beliefs which in turn leads to negative and destructive behaviour!

Here's a question that will help you see the link between the three things. Do you think people who are driven by anger, fear, guilt, sadness or hurt would **'believe'** it's:

- OK to trust?
- OK to let go?
- OK to delegate?
- OK to look for the possibilities in every situation?
- OK to fail from time to time; and mistakes are simply lessons from which we can learn?

NO!

So it follows that, because they don't **'believe'** these things, it's **IMPOSSIBLE** for them to do them! But here's the really important point: successful leaders and managers **DO** believe them and **would DO** them!

So we all need to be prepared to work on our self image and self esteem and if you don't know where to start, you might like to try a Paul McKenna book called **'Change Your Life in 7 Days'.** Forget any images you may have about Paul McKenna and his stage shows and:

- **Read** the book;
- **Do** the simple exercises;
- **Listen to the CD** that comes FREE with the book every day for a month.

If you do, I promise you'll find a **massive** difference: in the way you feel, the way you behave and the way people respond to you.

If you'd like a copy you'll find a link for the book, and the CD that comes with it, on the 7 Expensive Mistakes website.

I remember how badly I needed help with my self image before I could make my business work, so I **know** how important this is, but you must realise:

- Buying the book **isn't enough;**
- Just reading the book **isn't enough;**

- You have to **take action;**
- **Listen** to the CD daily;
- **Do** the exercises.

Do all this and you'll find everything becomes possible.

By the way, reading and listening to Paul McKenna isn't the **<u>only</u>** way you can improve your self image, it just happens to be the way that worked for me. If you'd like to explore the alternatives, look on Google using the search terms **'low self esteem'**, or **'poor self image'** and you'll find plenty to choose from.

Let's move on now to another important lesson we can learn from watching this clip.

To make change that lasts needs discipline.

Think about it:

- You need **discipline** to buy the book I've just recommended;
- You need **discipline** to read it;
- You need **discipline** to listen to the CD;
- You need **discipline** to do the exercises.

For all these things you need **<u>self</u>** discipline. But you're not the **<u>only</u>** one. If your business is going to grow, your team need to respond in a disciplined way as well and the cornerstone of discipline is a set of **<u>rules</u>.** Do you think Gordon Ramsay has a set of rules he runs his businesses with?

YOU BET HE DOES!

If you've watched the clip you'll remember, near the beginning when he got in the taxi, he said a rude word *(no surprise there!)* then he said: ***"I forgot to tell them about rule number 9".***

What's the lesson for us? Quite simply, far too many salons don't have a clear set of rules. They **<u>think</u>** they do, but they're not written down and aren't applied consistently, which leads to all sorts of problems. I'm not saying **'you'** have to write the rules on your own, without consulting your staff. If members of your team have the right attitude and suitable experience they absolutely **must** be involved in helping you create them. But once you've created the rules, everyone must sign to say they understand them and agree to stick to them.

By the way this applies to you too!

In his book **'The E Myth Revisited'** *(a must read book; you can find out more on the 7 Expensive Mistakes website)* the author **Michael E Gerber** makes the point that as the owner of the salon you have two different roles.

1. Working **'on'** your business: *This means making strategic decisions to ensure it's got the investment, training and resources it needs to carry on growing.*

2. Working **'in'** your business: *This means doing clients and carrying out your day to day leadership and management functions.*

Can you see the difference? Michael then goes on to say that when you're working **'in'** your business you absolutely **MUST** abide by the same rules and standards you expect your staff to work to.

- Now you might find this hard to believe, but I've seen salon owners who don't allow staff to use mobile phones in the salon ***keep their own phone with them while they're working on the floor.***

- I've seen salon owners who quite rightly don't allow staff to drink coffee on the salon floor ***keep a cup on the side for themselves, and think its 'OK' because it's their salon.***

BUT IT'S NOT OK!

If you think you're **'above the law'** and that the rules don't apply to you when you're working alongside your staff, you're asking for trouble, **GREAT BIG HEAPS OF IT**, because you'll end up with an **'us and them'** culture!

If this is ringing bells for you, take a careful look at which of your salon rules you're breaking at the moment because you think it's **'OK'!**

I'm sure you've got the point, so let's move on.

Rules are great because they give everyone rights and **responsibilities.** They give you the chance to reward the people who stick to them, and make sure there are consequences for the people who break them. But there's something beyond rules we need to think about as well.

We need to think about **standards.**

What's the difference between a rule and a standard? Rules simply state what you can and can't do. Standards define how well something needs to be done. They are the next step, if you like, and you'd better think about this carefully when you're creating your salon's rules.

You need to define the standard of performance you want from your stylists, covering things like:

- How many clients they should do;
- Their average bill;
- Total sales;
- Retail sales;
- Client retention and so on.

You need to define your acceptable standards of dress and etiquette, which would cover things like:

- Punctuality;
- Politeness;
- Consideration for the needs of others;
- Uniform or dress code ;
- Standards of personal appearance and so on.

You need to define your acceptable standard of attitude and we'll be looking at this in more detail later in the book.

You need to be very clear what the rewards are for those who meet and exceed your standards, and what the consequences are for those who don't! You have to measure your team's performance and behaviour against your standards fairly and consistently, so you know what's happening. Finally you have to act as an impartial referee and decide when a goal's been scored by your team and when a yellow or red card is needed!

> **Fact: If your 'self image' is strong enough you'll find it easy to create and referee a fair and effective set of rules and standards.**
>
> **Fact: If your 'self image' is weak you'll struggle to create and referee a fair and effective set of rules and standards.**

This is because, having a poor self image creates a power vacuum, and with it an unwritten invitation for other people to come in and undermine everything you try and do. You literally, **but unknowingly,** invite people to give you a hard time!

- Some salon owners try filling their vacuum and regaining control by nagging, or by being very strict.
- Others try and do it with **bribery** by giving extra attention, status, flattery, incentives, or money to the people who are undermining them and causing all the problems.
- **I also see them make the massive mistake of taking the good people around them for granted, just because they're not causing trouble!**

Do any of these strategies help?

No!

None of them get to the root of the problem, so while they may appear to have a short term effect, they don't work for long and they nearly always create more problems than they solve! So rule number 1 is work on improving your self image first, before you try and build your team or grow your business.

Breaking this rule is a very expensive mistake!

Don't forget you can see the 'Ramsay's Kitchen Nightmares' clip, and read more about 'Change Your Life in 7 Days' and 'The E Myth Revisited' by going to **www.7expensivemistakes.com**

"I could never have done it, before reading this book."

"This book is written in a language hairdressers will easily understand. Every salon owner or future salon owner now has a foolproof guide to achieving their goal. I'm already using the ideas suggested and I really feel I've regained control of my business.

*Salon owners may feel '**on their own**' and find themselves thinking ... "**who do I speak to, who else understands my problems?"** Not me ... **not anymore!** I now have my own business consultant right here with me all the time with this book!.*

I used to be the hairdresser who was tied to the back of the chair, no lunch breaks, no holidays, running around thinking only I could do it!

NOW I run my business with an amazing team, growing clientele and a vision. I could never have done it before reading this book ... so thank you Simon!"

Donna Finn. Male Ego Hair Salon

Expensive Mistake Number 2
Thinking it's 'OK' to be the weakest link ... because you're the BOSS!

'The Weakest Link' is another popular show with lessons to teach us.

The first, is that the set up of the show is surprisingly similar in one way to the set up of our salons. What **'way'** could that be? It's simple. As Anne Robinson says in her introduction, the contestants have to work together as a **team** to build the value of the ultimate prize; just as your stylists have to work together for the good of your salon. But at the same time the contestants in the show are competing **'against'** each other to win; just like your stylists compete **'against'** each other for clients and to be the most successful.

The tension this mix creates can be very healthy, but for this to happen, it needs to be managed well by a leader who has a positive self image and the ability to communicate. They can promote the benefits of working together and encourage everyone to feed off the spark a friendly rivalry can create.

I'll share with you my ***"SOS"*** *system* method for doing this a bit later in the book, but for the moment I'd like you to imagine what it would be like if you tried **'motivating'** a team by behaving like Anne Robinson does. What would happen if you played people off against each other, or used sarcasm, put downs and sneering ridicule like she does: **the results would be disastrous, wouldn't they!**

You'd end up with: a bitchy staff room, high staff turnover and problem after problem to deal with, **which wouldn't be great.**

Although this insight is important, it isn't the one I want to focus on in this chapter. Instead, to help us learn **'expensive mistake number 2'** I want to talk about a short compilation clip of 2005 X Factor contestant, Chico Slimani, taking part in a celebrity edition of the show. Don't forget, if you want to watch it, you can see the clip on the 7 Expensive Mistakes website.

You may remember Chico, he was the **'John and Edward'** of his day: limited talent, immense charm and a large personality. Simon Cowell hated him at the auditions and was furious when the other judges put him through; but in the end even Simon was won over by Chico's infectious enthusiasm.

Does that sound familiar?

He had his own catch phrase: "**It's Chico time**" which he and the musical director used as the title of a song they wrote together. Chico sang it on the show. Even now, nearly 5 years later, it's still the only time an original song has been sung on **'The X Factor'** by a contestant and it went down really well.

Although Chico only came 5th in the end, he did get the chance to release **'Its Chico time'** as a single afterwards and it went on to be number 1 in the charts and stayed there for 2 weeks. His appearance on **'The Weakest Link'** has all the Chico trademark charm, but as we see in both the rounds he takes part in: *'he is the weakest link.'*

So what's this got to do with salon owners and **'expensive mistake number 2'**? Well, the name of the show comes from the saying: "A chain is only as strong as its weakest link." When Chico's playing to his strengths, he's very strong, but take him out of his comfort zone and despite his efforts to gloss over his poor performance, we can see he's weak.

The same lesson applies to us as salon owners when it comes to the discipline of managing our salons and leading our staff. Most of us are **very** talented at doing certain things. When we stick to them, we can fly, just like Chico. But no matter how talented any of us may be at doing some things we're only **'average'** and way outside our comfort zone doing others: **just like Chico!**

Every time we're 'average' at leadership or management we run the risk of being 'the weakest link' in our salon and when times get tough, such as during a recession, the weakness will be exposed and you'll pay a heavy price.

Just like Chico, a lot of salon owners try and cover their weaknesses with bulls**t and charm, but it doesn't change the fact that the business is probably going to suffer if it isn't run properly. This is a big enough risk to cause most of us very expensive problems but many salon owners are prepared to take an even **BIGGER** risk.

They're prepared to miss 'average' out all together and completely **avoid** certain parts of their leadership or management responsibilities because they either:

- Don't **want** to do it because it makes them feel uncomfortable;
- Think they can't **afford** to do it;
- Don't think they **need** to do it;
- Don't know **how** to do it;
- Or think it doesn't matter because they're the **boss**.

But it does matter and whatever the reason is ... they're making a BIG MISTAKE! Let me explain. If we stick with the "a chain is only as strong as its weakest link" concept for a moment, imagine each link in the chain represents a different area of leadership or management responsibility within your salon.

As a minimum your chain should have every single one of the following links in it:

- *Marketing;*
- *Stock Control;*
- *Accounts/Wages/Admin;*
- *Health and safety;*
- *Staff recruitment;*
- *Staff training;*
- *Staff motivation;*
- *Artistic leadership;*
- *Customer service;*
- *Property maintenance;*
- *Strategic planning.*

Why?

Because they're **all** critical parts of your business, *(that's what I discovered* *as I developed my **"SOS"** system)* and as the salon owner you're responsible for making sure your business does them **ALL** properly!

The important question is: "Which are you good at and which do you do badly, or ignore completely until a problem hits you **'SLAP'** right in the face?"

You need to answer this question, so go back to the list and look at it again with honesty. You must decide which activities play to your strengths and which bore you, frustrate you, or scare you.

When you've finished going through the list you simply need to focus on two things.

1. **Actively taking responsibility for the areas that play to your strengths.**
2. **Finding a way to get the others done by people who are equipped to do them well ... In other words DELEGATING THEM!**

You're probably thinking ... that sounds great Simon, I know I should do it **but I don't know how!** You'll be relieved to know you'll discover lots of tips on **'how'** all the way through this book.

SO DO READ IT ALL!

But the really good news is, we've already covered the first **'how'** step when we looked at **'expensive mistake number 1'** which, I'm sure you'll remember, encouraged you to work on building a positive self image and high self esteem. But here's something you need to understand.

Fact: People with a poor self image find it very hard to delegate effectively. People with a strong self image do it easily.

Fact: If you don't learn to delegate you'll never grow your business beyond a certain limited size and you'll certainly feel like you're stuck in a 'RUT' while you're running it.

So now you probably realise that **'expensive mistakes number 1 and 2'** are linked and you can't fix number 2 until you've fixed number 1, *although lots of salon owners try and then wonder why it doesn't work!*

Here's another question for you to think about: Did you find it **'easy'** to go through that list of activities a few minutes ago and sort out what **'you'** should do and what you should delegate?

If you didn't, it's absolutely essential that you get to know yourself better, so you can play to your strengths in future and reduce the chance of becoming the **'The Weakest Link'** in your salon! To help you build a clearer picture of *'what you're naturally good at'* we're going to do a simple exercise taken from my ***"SOS"*** *system*. I also use a book with my clients as I take them through the system, called **STRENGTHS FINDER 2** written by Tom Wrath. The great thing about this book is that it comes with the password for an on line diagnostic test you can take which automatically produces a detailed report of your **5 top strengths.**

Remember taking the **STRENGTHS FINDER 2** online diagnostic test is in addition to the exercise I want you to do right now; so grab a pencil and either write down your answers in the book or if you'd rather, you can download an answer sheet from the 7 Expensive Mistakes website.

Let's make a start.

- **Are you naturally tidy ... or untidy?**

  I am ______________________

- **Which is more important to you security: or freedom?**

  I think ____________________ is more important

- **Do you need 'to do' lists, wall planners and a personal organ iser to function: or are you happier just writing things down on the nearest scrap of paper and filing stuff in piles?**

  I prefer ____________________

- **Are you an 'always on time' person: or a 'just about on time' some of the time person.**

  I am ____________________________

- **Are you an 'ideas' person who spends lots of time day dreaming: or a people person who craves the company and contact of others all the time?**

  I am ____________________________

- **Are you good at starting things and then you get bored so most of them don't get finished: or are you determined to finish what you start, no matter what?**

  I am ____________________________

Have you answered every question? Has it helped you to see what you need some help with? I hope so, but let me see if I can make it even clearer for you!

A salon needs to be tidy. Why? Because at least 40% of the population are totally turned off by a dirty or untidy environment. **You can't afford to turn off that many people.** If being tidy doesn't come naturally to you, you'll be a weak link in your salon and it will hold back the development of your business, so it makes sense to get someone who is **naturally** tidy to take responsibility!

The vast majority of your staff and clients crave the security of knowing where they stand, what they can expect and how they fit in. In other words, they like routine, they like structure and they like consistency.

If you love freedom and the flexibility to change your mind whenever you feel like it, you'll find it hard to communicate and deliver an experience that makes the people around you feel secure. The danger is they'll go somewhere else looking for security and your business won't grow.

So if you're very flexible by nature and freedom is more important than security, you'll be a weak link in the development of your salon. This means it makes sense to get someone who values security to organise you **and** manage your business to make sure your people are given the security they need!

A salon needs to be well organised with rules, systems and proper records. This helps everyone be clear about what's expected of them, helps you measure everyone's contribution consistently and it also protects **you** from unwanted problems if anything needs investigating in future.

If you're not a naturally organised person who's good at keeping records, planning for meetings and getting the right things done at the right time, you'll be a weak link in the development of your business. So get someone who's good at record keeping and running systems to do it for you!

A salon needs to run to a time schedule. If you're someone who finds this difficult, you'll be seen as unreliable, inconsistent and some people will find it hard to trust you. If other people's time isn't important to you, you'll be a weak link in the growth of your business, so give someone permission to manage your time for you and remind you where you have to be **and when!**

It's great to be creative and come up with good ideas that can take your business forward; but it's also important that your people feel cared for, appreciated and nurtured. Very few people can do both well, so do what you're good at and ***get some help with the rest!***

It's great if you're good at starting things, but they need to be finished as well. Very few people can do both consistently, so do what you're good at and ***get some help with the rest!***

Are you getting the message?

Very few of us are good at everything, but your business needs someone to be responsible for **everything** and it's an expensive mistake to be responsible for things we don't enjoy or take pride in doing well.

When I first understood this, I thought "I'm only a small business, I haven't got a lot of staff, I can't afford to employ lots of outsiders. **HELP!"** But then I took a deep breath, thought about it and started making some changes. I got members of my family to help. My mother in law kept my weekly record sheets for me, my father in law did my accounts, my sister did my newsletter and in return **I did their hair for free!** You must have friends, family or clients with skills you can barter your hairdressing for.

I also held a meeting with the 4 staff I had at the time and gave them a sheet with 4 areas of responsibility listed on it:

- Stock control.
- Window/retail display.
- Time management.
- Salon maintenance.

I asked them to give **4 points** to the team member they thought would be best at managing each responsibility, **3 points** to the second best, **2 points** to the third and **1point** to the last person.

I voted as well, but my name wasn't on the list because my job was to help all of them. When we added up all the points, we found a different person had scored highest for each responsibility.

I then asked each person if they were happy to take responsibility for that role. Because they'd been paid the compliment of being chosen as the best, they all said yes and they **all** did a very good job! My role was to simply make sure they had the training, resources, support and encouragement to do well and then get out of their way ***and let them do it!*** I was then set free to concentrate on the things **'I'** did well and the business has never looked back!

By the way, if you get addicted to the idea of discovering even more about yourself, *which I recommend you do,* have a look at **'Personality 100'** the most comprehensive **'on line personality assessment'** you can take. As always, there's a link on the 7 Expensive Mistakes website.

I recommend you keep learning about yourself because it gives you the knowledge you need to build on your known strengths and delegate round your weaknesses. Doing this gives you the freedom to take control of your business **and ignoring this fact is a very expensive mistake!**

By the way, I understand that some of this will be way outside your comfort zone and might seem a bit of a challenge, so if the thought of organising the:

- *Marketing;*
- *Health and safety;*
- *Staff recruitment;*
- *Staff training;*
- *Staff motivation;*
- *Artistic leadership;*
- *Customer service ;*
- *and Strategic planning responsibilities;*

in your salon seems a bit daunting, you might want to take a closer look at my ***"SOS"*** *system* which gives you all the tools and support you could need to create a well organised and profitable salon! You'll find more details in the last chapter - when you're ready, have a look.

Remember you can see 'The Weakest Link' clip, find out more about 'Strengths Finder 2' and 'Personality 100' and download the exercise I gave you at **www.7expensivemistakes.com**

"The absolute foundation for building a successful business."

"The most amazing insight for me was the advice on self-belief and confidence, and how it's linked to success ... a subject which is tackled superbly in the book.

Understanding this has become to me the absolute foundation for building a successful business.

Without strong foundations the rest of the building could come tumbling down at any moment ... and I think a lot of salon owners don't realise their foundation (inner-belief) may be lacking and should be tackled first.

Through this book that can absolutely be achieved."

Amanda Quinn, Eden Hairdressing

Expensive Mistake Number 3
Putting up with 'Hyacinth' when you don't have to!

So far in this book the focus has been on **you,** hasn't it! I've shown you how important it is to work on your self image and also to make sure you play to your strengths. When you do, you'll find things will begin improving rapidly for you.

In this chapter we're going to give you a break by looking at the people you have around you instead and the difference they can make to getting you in or out of your **'RUT'**. The TV programme that's going to help us this time is the sitcom from the 1990's called **'Keeping Up Appearances'**

Don't forget, if you want to watch it, you can see the clip on the 7 Expensive Mistakes website.

Now as you may remember the main character in the series is a formidable lady called **Hyacinth Bucket** *who insists on pronouncing it* ***BOUQUET!*** The programme is very funny because Hyacinth causes havoc and chaos in the lives of everyone around her. You can see the reason for this is because she has a very poor self image, and she's desperate to hide behind a screen of **'sophisticated appearances'** to try and make her feel **'OK'** about herself.

Remember Hyacinth is only an example of **'one'** type of low self esteem or poor self image behaviour; as we saw earlier *there are many that can be just as damaging.* But, bless her, she's going to teach us the very important lesson that it's just as dangerous and expensive to employ people with a poor self image as it is to try to run a business **if your own 'self image' is poor!**

In the clip I've chosen, we see her deciding to go out for a drive with her downtrodden husband. He obviously wants to keep her happy so he panders to her every whim:

- He makes sure the car is spotless and ready for inspection so she looks good when they're seen in public.
- He asks her which route she wants to take and obediently complies without complaint when she changes her mind 3 times, because he

doesn't want to be nagged.

- He tolerates it when she tells him he's going too fast, when she thinks he hasn't seen a cyclist, or a lorry parked on the other side of the dual carriageway and so on!

Does his constant compliance make her happy? **NO!** And it never will!

What's this got to do with you? It's simple. You own or manage a salon. The success of the salon is your responsibility. You're the leader; you're the boss, **the buck stops with you.**

You're like the driver of a car. You have the controls. You have the responsibility. A car can carry passengers. So can your business because your staff, your clients, your suppliers, your backers or partners can all be thought of as passengers.

The important question is: Do they all want to go where you're going, or are any of them behaving like Hyacinth? Are they trying to make themselves feel better by getting you to run your salon to their agenda?"

If any of them are trying to hijack your agenda, **what effect does it have on you?** Does it help you make smooth progress on your journey to where you plan to go, or does it end up causing friction, endless problems and make you feel like you're going round in circles or getting completely lost?

Fact: It's your decision whether a Hyacinth gets in your car.

Fact: It's your decision whether she stays in your car.

In other words, it's your decision whether you remain in control of your business and are surrounded by the right people, or are **'driven to distraction'** by passengers who undermine you, nag you, bully you or simply ignore your wishes because they couldn't give a **** about what you want.

Please get the point I'm making here: **If you have staff members or a partner who are trying to control or disrupt your business for their own agenda, rather than helping you with yours, you need to look at ways of getting them out before you get completely lost.**

By the way I'm not saying these are **'bad'** people, in another environment they may be fine. It's just that like a round peg doesn't fit into a square hole, they don't **'fit'** with you and what you're trying to do in your business!

Here's a simple exercise from my ***"SOS"*** *system* to help you identify any 'Hyacinths' that might be keeping you in your **'RUT'.**

If you've got access to a computer you can download the sheet for this exercise from the website. If not, just get a piece of paper and make a list of the names of everyone you employ or who's involved in any way with helping you run your salon.

When you've done that, take each name on your list in turn, and based on your experience of working with them, ask yourself the following **4** questions ... *(Go with your gut reaction when you're doing this exercise and take no more than* ***5*** *seconds to answer any of the questions.)*

Question 1.

Does this person have an attitude I'm comfortable with, and the skills to do the job I want?

YES or NO

Question 2.

Does this person have an attitude I'm comfortable with, but their skills need improving to get to the right level?

YES or NO

Question 3.

Does this person have an attitude I find frustrating and challenging but has the skills needed to do the job well?

YES or NO

Question 4.

Does this person have an attitude I find frustrating and challenging, and their skills need improving to get to the right level?

YES or NO

*Each time you ask this series of questions, the person concerned should end up with **3 'No's'** and **1 'Yes'** as answers, and all I want you to do is make a note of the **number** of the question you answered **'Yes'** to, next to their name on the list.*

When you do this exercise properly you should finish with a list of names, and next to each name will be the number of the question you answered **'YES'** to. Is that what you've got? **GREAT!**

What shall we do with the information?

Ask yourself, who deserves your time, energy, support and encouragement:

The people who are supporting you and have an attitude you can work with?

Or the people who frustrate you, and want to pull you in different directions to suit their own agenda?

The answer is obvious isn't it! You work with those that want to work with **you** and they're the people who've got a number 1 or number 2 next to their name on your list. What's not so obvious is this: instead of trying to bribe or motivate your 'Hyacinths' to change their behaviour... ***just do 2 things:***

Every time they break a rule or cause a problem, take them to one side and in a quiet, non emotional, **professional** manner, tell them what they've done wrong, explain it's unacceptable and be very clear what the consequences will be if they do it again.

Every time they do something positive that you want to encourage, **pay them the compliment of noticing and saying well done**.

The rest of the time you simply **ignore** them except for the usual day to day need to be polite and work together.

> **Fact: Only someone with a positive self image will be able to do this consistently, but if you do manage it, one of two things will happen very quickly:**

They'll get fed up because their tactics aren't working anymore and leave.

They'll modify their behaviour to get more of the praise they now deserve and you won't want them to leave!

Either way you win!

Ignoring **'expensive mistake number 3'** will not only cost you a lot of money but years of frustration and heartache as well!

Now; if you think back to the beginning of the last chapter when we talked about **'the weakest link'**, I promised to share with you the ***"SOS"*** *system* method I developed to create a team that's happy to work **'with'** each other and compete **'against'** each other at the same time.

I didn't give it to you earlier because employing a 'Hyacinth' would make it impossible for you to copy the method and you needed to understand that before it would all make sense:

The first principle you need to follow to use the method successfully is this: **Everyone** on your team should be equal when it comes to their right to be treated with respect and dignity. There must be no 'status' driven, 'dead men's shoes' pecking order. Everyone should be allowed to contribute what they are capable of, to whatever task or project needs doing at the time, and be **respected** for it.

The second principle is this: Everyone should be allowed to grow at their own pace, as long as they follow the rules. It's also important that their work ethic and attitude is in line with your well defined and measured standards.

The third principle is this: The stylists who take the most money should be the best paid, and be properly **recognised** for what they achieve. It's only fair to reward excellence and achievement after all. The important thing is that everyone else in your team should know that the only thing stopping them from earning more and being recognised as well is **their attitude, their behaviour and their results.** In other words it's equality of **opportunity** you offer with this method, not equality of **outcome.**

If you organise your team using these principles, you give **every** member a sense of being important and feeling trusted, from an early stage.

The idea is based on the Three Musketeers motto **'All for one and one for all'.** If you work with your team in this way they'll repay you by happily taking on a lot of responsibility, very quickly and they'll do it well. Creating **'All for one and one for all'** gave me my freedom and grew my salon quickly. In other words, it's how I got out of my **'RUT'!**

The **6** steps to successfully creating **'All for one and one for all'** are easy. In fact we've already covered them while we've been talking about the first **3** expensive mistakes. Here's a quick reminder for you; have a look and you'll see how they all fit together:

Step 1. Work on improving your self image.

Step 2. As it improves you'll find you'll learn to trust and accept yourself.

Step 3. Then you'll feel able to trust and accept others for who they are and what they can offer.

Step 4. Then you'll feel comfortable delegating things to them.

Step 5. Then you'll have the freedom to **'only'** do the things you enjoy and are good at.

Step 6. Then you'll find it easy to see who **'fits'** in your team and who doesn't ***and create an 'All for one and one for all' team.***

If you've been reading the testimonials and comments at the start of each chapter, you'll know that following these steps to create **'All for one and one for all'** has worked not only for me, but many other salon owners as well, young and old, male and female, experienced and inexperienced. ***And they're not the only ones who feel strongly about this!***

My team are passionate about **'All for one and one for all'** because it makes them feel 'special' and 'important' so they guard it fiercely. If you create an **'All for one and one for all'** team, I promise they will feel the same.

If I take on a new employee who turns out to be a 'Hyacinth' my team let me know **very** quickly and they trust me to act decisively to move the new person on; your team will do the same for you. If they didn't behave in this way our teams would gradually self destruct, and that's the last thing we'd want, isn't it!

All this makes the interviewing process critically important, so that is what we'll talk about next! Before we do, there's one last principle I want you to understand.

'All for one and one for all' applies to the team, **not you!**

If you want them to take responsibility it's got to feel like it's **'their'** team not yours. For the method to work you **have** to work with them, of course, but from the **outside**. This means it's important you realise, they don't have to **'like'** you but they do have to **'respect'** you. That's why **you** must treat all of them with respect and make sure you obey the same rules you ask them to obey.

Another way of looking at this is to see yourself as the **'parent'** of your team, not as a child within it, if that makes sense.

As the **'parent'** you should nurture, educate, appreciate and discipline your team members. Do this and you'll help them to grow into a strong, independent group, who'll trust you and take responsibility for their own success. I'm sure you've realised by now, you can only play the **'parent'** role consistently, ***if you have a positive self image.***

Remember you can see the 'Keeping Up Appearances' clip and download a copy of the 'Hyacinth' finder exercise from my ***"SOS"*** *system* at **www.7expensivemistakes.com**

"Since I started using the knowledge in this book I find myself becoming the employer I always wanted to be."

"When I started my salon, all I ever wanted was to create a workspace where people, who love hairdressing as much as I do are appreciated and allowed to grow ... but for reasons I didn't understand ... it wasn't working.

My big ***AHA*** *moment with this book came when it struck me that my employees (loyal and hard working) are looking at me to be the one thing I tried to avoid being ...*

THE BOSS!

I now realise my employees don't need me to be their friend or let them do as they please in the salon. To my surprise they prefer to have rules to follow, and guidelines to stick to.

I'm delighted to say since I started using the knowledge in this book I find myself becoming the employer I always wanted to be."

Pamela Laird, Finn and Co

Expensive Mistake Number 4
Employing the wrong people!

In the last chapter we learned how costly it is to try and work with people whose self image takes their behaviour in a direction we're not comfortable with.

I've already mentioned that business owners with a poor self image and low self esteem seem to attract **'trouble'** people, and they seem to find it difficult to cope when it happens. However, high self esteem employers **do** take on the wrong people as well from time to time, either because they're too busy, or don't know how, to interview properly. **It's just that once they realise there's a problem with a new employee, they deal with it decisively and the problem goes away.**

I heard one describe it once as our **"fit in or **** off"** policy, which sums it up rather nicely! But, wouldn't it be better if we never took on these people in the first place? Wouldn't it be better if we had a clear picture of the self image, beliefs, values and attitude of the person we're thinking of employing, ***before we offered them a job?***

Well the good news is, when we're interviewing we can put on a pair of magic glasses and see right through the person we're interviewing: ***if we follow a simple set of rules!***

When you realise how much it costs to sort out the mess a poor hiring decision can create for you, you'd think we'd all be rushing off to learn these rules!

But we don't.

Instead we think **"I'll get round to it sometime"** but right now I need to *(insert your excuse here)* instead.

THIS IS AN EXPENSIVE MISTAKE.

The TV clip I've chosen to illustrate **'expensive mistake number 4'** is taken from a day time TV game show called **'Golden Balls'** which is hosted by Jasper Carrot. Don't forget, if you want to watch it, you can see the clip on the website.

We join them towards the end of the show at the point called **'Split or Steal'.** The **2** remaining contestants are given **2** Golden Balls each. When they open them they can see that one ball contains the word **'Split'**, the other contains the word **'Steal'**.

Jasper explains the rules and asks the contestants to choose either their **'Split'** or **'Steal'** ball in secret, knowing that their choice has one of the following consequences:

- If they both choose **'Split'** the prize money is shared and they get half each.
- If they both choose **'Steal'** the prize money is lost to both of them.
- If one of them chooses **'Split'** and the other chooses **'Steal'** the stealer takes **ALL** the money and the splitter gets **NOTHING!**

Once he's explained the rules Jasper gives the contestants time to talk to each other so they can discuss their intentions and feelings. Each contestant uses the information they get from talking to make a decision about what they're going to do. I think this point of the game is rather like a job interview where the employer and prospective employee make promises to each other which they:

- *Both might keep;*
- *One might keep and the other break ;*
- *They both might break!*

By the way this particular show is a little different to normal because both the contestants have been on the show before. They've been invited back for a second chance because both of them were let down last time when they decided to **'Split'** and their opponent **'Stole'** the money from them. As you'll see, their previous bad experience has damaged them. It has a profound effect on what they say to each other and what they finally decide to do.

The same thing often happens at interviews. Employers become cynical and scarred after a few bad hiring experiences; and so do staff who've had a series of disappointing bosses. This can lead to either of them choosing the strategy of saying whatever they think the other person needs to hear during the interview ***just to get the result they want.***

Anyway, back to the show, it's nail biting stuff, especially as the prize pot they're playing for is over **£100,000** which is life changing money!

Look carefully at the contestants and you'll see: promises being made, promises being **'suggested'** but not actually made, ***you'll see all sorts of interesting body language,*** but can you guess beforehand who is going to choose to do what?

I'd love you to pause the clip, just before the contestants reveal their balls and decide what you think is going to happen. As soon as you've decided ... press play and see if you were right! I won't spoil the surprise by revealing the answer but, like me, you'll probably feel it's almost shocking and certainly not fair.

The same thing is true if we don't interview properly and end up making a bad hiring decision: ***so it's important to have a set of rules to help us interview well, isn't it!***

We need rules that give your candidate reliable information, *and if the truth about your salon is so unattractive that it would put a candidate off if you spilled the beans, you'd better sort that out before you recruit anyone else!*

We need rules that make it almost impossible for candidates to avoid revealing their true **'self'** to you.

Well here they are!

Follow the rules I'm about to share and you'll find, both you and your candidate will be in the position to make an informed decision. You're also far more likely to form a mutually profitable working partnership.

Before I get to the specific rules here are four guiding principles to follow:

1. **Conduct your interviews in the 'right' frame of mind:** *It's so important not to be* ***desperate****. One of my favourite sayings is:* ***"It's better to have no staff than the wrong staff."***

2. **Hire slowly and fire quickly:** *Take the time to interview candidates thoroughly, then give your staff the chance to meet them and express an opinion as well, before you finally decide whether to offer a 3 month trial period or not* ***and if you have any doubts or concerns during those first 3 months, take that as a sign, let them go and be prepared to start again.***

3. **Don't take anything you're told at face value**: *Use it as a starting point for further discussion* ***and that's it!***

4. **Know what you're looking for:** *You must understand that getting a feeling for a candidate's self image, attitudes, beliefs and values is* ***far*** *more important to you than a picture of their current skill level: This is simply because it's much easier to train the 'right' person to become a good hairdresser* ***than it is to train a good hairdresser to become the 'right' person for your team.***

Follow these principles and you won't go far wrong. Now let's move on to the rules I promised you:

1. Start with a suitable venue that sets the right tone. Don't use your staff room or anywhere that you can be interrupted.

2. If you don't have a suitable place in your salon, use a local hotel. I've held many interviews in hotel lounges and I've found as long as you buy tea or coffee at regular intervals they're quite happy for you to be there.

3. How and where you sit is important; so to help you get your body language right, sit at the same level as the person you're interviewing with no barriers between you and preferably at a 90 degree angle to them.

4. Start the interview with a brief scene setting speech, which makes lots of points that they would naturally agree with *and nod a couple of times every few seconds while you're saying it to promote agrement.*

5. It might seem strange, but to help them relax your speech should be **'hypnotic'** in quality, *which means long sentences that are slightly confusing but hard to disagree with.* An example of this would be ... ***"You've come here today for an interview*** *(nod nod)* ***because you're interested in joining our team*** *(nod nod)* ***and if we're both going to make the right decision it's important we talk openly to each other, isn't it,*** *(nod nod)* ***so let's just relax, take our time, and see what happens*** *(nod nod)* ***..now tell me ..."*** and off you go!

6. Remember, while we're interviewing, what we're **really** looking to discover are the beliefs, attitudes and values that make them **'who'** they are.

7. The secret to doing this is combining my **'magic mirror'** technique with some simple questions. Learn to use these together and interviewing will become **very** easy for you!

We'll get to the questions in a moment, but remember, on their own, they **don't** have the magic we're looking for. You absolutely must combine them with my **'magic mirror'** technique to make them work.

Here's the first step to using my **'magic mirror'** technique:

When you both sit down at the beginning of the interview ... ***sit like they do.***

If they:

a. Fold their arms: ***fold your arms;***

b. Cross their legs: ***cross your legs;***

c. Sit upright: ***sit upright yourself;***

d. Slouch: ***slouch yourself;***

e. Lean towards you: ... ***lean towards them, and so on.***

Then for the first two minutes **'mirror'** any changes they make in how they sit. We do this to make them feel comfortable; and if you want to see a short demonstration of mirroring, you'll find a clip of one just underneath the **'Golden Balls'** clip on the 7 Expensive Mistakes website.

Here's the second step to using my **'magic mirror'** technique:

When an interviewee answers a question you must ***ALWAYS*** listen carefully to:

1. **'What'** they are saying: *does it fit with what's on their CV, what they've already told you and what they **'look'** like; and we'll **'look'** at that in more detail in a second.*

2. **'How'** they are saying it: *does their voice change, do they sound louder or quieter, do they start to mumble or stumble, do they get **'excited'** or go flat.*

By the way, becoming a good listener is easy if you follow a simple rule, which is: *"don't think about what you're going to say next, **just watch and listen until they've finished talking!"***

Watch for:

1. A change of expression on their face: ***they may smile, raise an eye brow, blush or go white.***

2. A change of posture: ***they may sit back, sit forward, lean towards or lean away from you, cross or uncross their arms or legs.***

3. A gesture with their hands: ***they may point at something imaginary, sit on their hands, make a chopping or pushing gesture. They may wave their hands about, touch their nose or mouth or scratch their head.***

All these changes can be a sign of a **'reaction'** and behind a reaction is an **'emotion'** and that's what you're after, because you're looking for what matters to **them.**

Here's the third step to using my **'magic mirror'** technique:

Using **your** **'magic mirror'** you must reflect their **'reaction'** back at them in a follow up question, to help you find out more about the **'emotion'** that might be behind the reaction you've spotted. Make sure you reflect the **same** word(s) and gesture(s) back to them when you ask your question.

For example, they might say that they **'hated'** being at school. *(As they say the word **'hated'** they might make a chopping gesture with their hand.)*

You could turn their reaction into a question like : "I can see you really meant it when you said you **'hated'** school *(and as you say the word **'hated'** you repeat the chopping gesture);* what happened to make you feel like that?"

Can you see, you're repeating part of what they said, in the same way they said it, but you've turned it into the form of a question.

Remember, reflecting language and gestures back to anyone you talk to, will give them the feeling you understand them deeply. This means they are far more likely to open up and tell you more. In fact, when you learn to reflect well, ***you'll get to know them much better than they really want you too!*** Don't forget, you've got **2** eyes, **2** ears and only **1** mouth, so listen and watch very carefully while you're reflecting **...** ***at least four times as much as you talk!***

WARNING!

When you first use the **'magic mirror'** technique it will probably feel uncomfortable and you'll think the other person knows what you're doing. It's quite **'normal'** to feel this way and I promise you the other person won't have a clue what's going on; and if you practice, practice, practice and get really comfortable using it, ***your life and your salon will never be the same again!***

Now before we get to the helpful questions I promised, I want you to remember that each one of them is only the starting point of a conversation you can have, a conversation you control because you're comfortable with the **'magic mirror'** technique.

If you find you're getting through all the questions in less than half an hour it's a sign that **you're not using the 'magic mirror' technique properly.**

If this happens, just practice until it becomes second nature and you'll find yourself talking less, listening more and asking better follow up questions, without even thinking about it!

By the way, the **'magic mirror'** technique and the interview questions are both part of my ***"SOS"*** *system.* You can download an interview sheet with the questions and a place to record your thoughts from the 7 Expensive Mistakes website.

Here are the questions so let's get started:

1. " If I was talking to your best friend, what **3** words do you think they might use to describe you?"

2. "Sometimes we're inspired by people we know, sometimes it's someone we read or hear about. I'm interested to know who you think has been the most inspiring person in your life."

3. "A recent survey showed that Hairdressers enjoy their job more than any other profession; what do you feel makes it so enjoyable?"

4. "If I gave you **£10,000** and said you had to spend it in the next **24hrs** what would you do with it?"

5. "If you join us, you'll be joining a team; how quickly would you see yourself fitting in?"

6. "Everyone in our team needs to be comfortable taking responsibility so I'd like you to give me an example of something you've done that shows you're a responsible person."

7. "Where do you see yourself in 10 years time?"

8. "If money was no object; what would you do on your perfect holiday?"

9. "Tell me about the last time you felt really successful."

10. "Give me 3 reasons why I should seriously consider giving you this opportunity!"

How do those questions feel to you? Can you see yourself using them successfully? Good.

Now, let's get back to the interview structure. If after you've had your **'magic mirror'** chat you're pretty sure the person isn't who you're looking for, simply thank them for coming and tell them you'll write and let them know your decision when you've finished interviewing.

If you think they have potential, pay them the compliment of saying so, and then ask: "What questions would you like to ask me?"

As you answer their questions, look for the right time to give them a clear picture of what they can expect if they're successful.

For example I'm always looking for the right opportunity to say:

> *"You must understand I'm not looking for someone who simply wants a job; I'm looking for someone who wants a* ***career****.*
>
> *If you're successful and join us you'll be given the opportunity, the tools and the environment to create a successful career, but, and it's a* ***BIG BUT****, whether you achieve it or not is up to* ***you****.*
>
> *Of course the team and I will be here to guide and help you, but we can't and* ***won't*** *do it for you; and if we* ***ever*** *get the feeling you're not committed to making the most of the opportunity, we'll be parting company:* ***now, do you still want to join us?"***

Do you know what? If they get this far, they always say YES! So ask yourself: "What would my version of that speech sound like?"

The final step I suggest you follow in the interviewing process is another simple exercise from my ***"SOS"*** *system*.

Give them 4 sheets of paper. Each one should have one of the following symbols on it; you'll find what you need on the ***"SOS"*** *system* interview sheets you can download from the 7 Expensive Mistakes website.

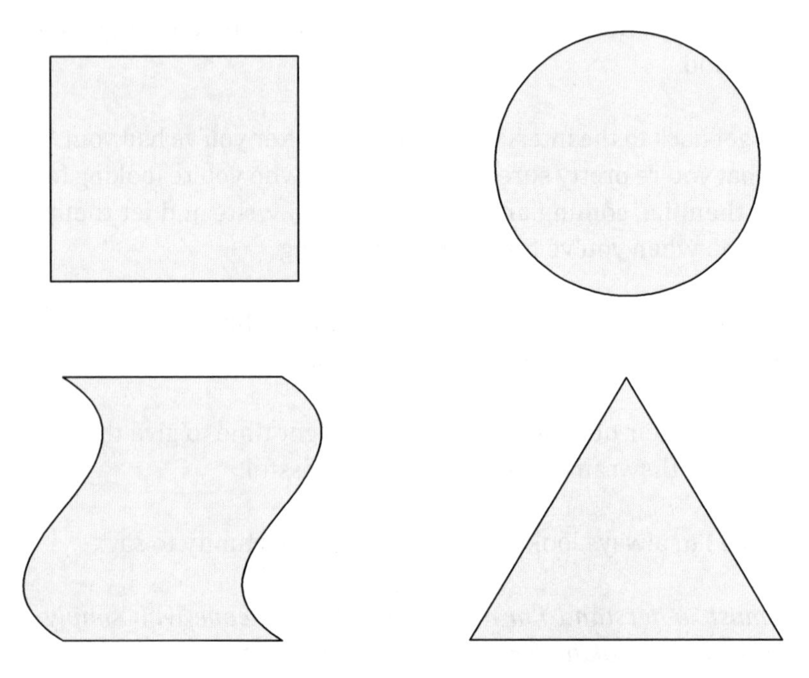

Ask them to put the sheets in order, with their favourite on the top, their second favourite next and so on. You'll find the **'order'** they choose tells you a lot about their priorities and what makes them tick.

But here's a word of warning.

This exercise is only about **80%** accurate, so **do** check your results by following up their selection with extra questions. I find the best way to check is to ask if they've ever done this exercise before, *which they rarely have* and then ask if they'd like you to explain what it all means: ***they always say yes!*** Then I tell them about the typical characteristics of the type of people who prefer each symbol, which are ***as follows.***

People who choose the square normally:

- Love detail;
- Make lists;
- Hate being late;
- Always tidy up and put things away after they finish using them.

People who choose the circle normally:

- Love people;
- Enjoy entertaining them;
- Like caring for them;
- Only feel complete when they're in the company of other people.

People who choose the squiggle normally:

- Love change;
- Hate being tied down;
- Are always changing their minds;
- Are often late;
- Are disorganised and untidy;
- But they do come up with great ideas!

People who choose the triangle normally:

- Are driven to get things done;
- Get to the point ;
- Are direct;
- Are focussed;
- Are competitive;
- Often don't care if they upset people.

I tell them that most of us are a **'combination'** of characteristics from 2 and sometimes 3 of the shapes; but we all have a dominant way of behaving. I then explain what the order of their choice suggests to me about **them** ... and then I ask whether what I've said is true or not, and I look for their reaction.

You can really have fun with this, because it doesn't matter whether what you've said **is** true or not! Why not? Because; either way, you'll find you can build on their reaction with your **'magic mirror'** technique and when you do, you'll discover more about what really makes them tick!

Just remember it doesn't matter which way you get to know them better, all that matters is ***you do get to know them better!***

When you've finished you then have to decide if they're good enough to go on to the next stage of your hiring process. For me, the next stage should always involve meeting and spending time with your team, so they can be part of the decision making process as well. If your candidate is going on to the next stage, let them know when they can expect to hear from you.

Hiring the wrong people can be a VERY expensive mistake. Don't do the 'same old, same old' interviews and don't fall for the 'Golden Balls' trap.

Remember, you can see the **'Golden Balls'** clip and download the ***"SOS"*** *system* interview sheets you'll be needing at **www.7expensivemistakes.com**

"This book should be called ... The Salon Owners bible."

"I love Simon's philosophy. He makes you realise your salons potential and guides you through the common pitfalls of the day to day running of a salon. It really changes the way you look at yourself, your staff and your business."

In my opinion this book should be called ... "The Salon Owners bible."

Sue Beardsmore, Profiles Hairdressing

Expensive Mistake Number 5
Running a 'JOKE' business!

Right: It's time to stop talking about people and start talking about the business of **'business'** but I promise I'll keep it simple, to the point and jargon free!

To help us we're going to look at one of the most enjoyable business TV programmes called **'Dragons Den'** but before we do I want to ask you a question about your salon.

In your mind, do you see it as a proper **'business'** or if you're being honest, is it just an alternative to a job, which you prefer because you want a bit more control?

Why am I asking?

Well, if you see it as a job, your priority will simply be making enough money to replace the wages you would earn if you were **'employed'.**

If you see it as a business, it **has** to do better than that. It has to make sense as an **'investment'** which means it's got to pay its staff properly *(including you)* **and** make a good return on investment as well.

That's what **'Dragons Den'** is all about - 5 very successful entrepreneurs looking to see if any of the businesses being presented to them make sense as an **'investment'** not just a job for its owner.

The clip I've selected to help you learn more about '**expensive mistake number 5'** is actually a 'joke' clip. Don't forget, if you want to watch it, you can see it on the 7 Expensive Mistakes website.

In it we see an inventor who's come up with an amazing gadget called the **'Frigaton 2000 Freeze Gun'** which he claims will freeze anything instantly. He then demonstrates that it works by freezing a whole chicken in front of the Dragons.

So far so good!

Despite the fact his invention works, he's then given a really hard time by the Dragons because he hasn't prepared the **'business'** case for his project and if there's one thing they can't stand it's someone making a pitch who hasn't prepared their business case.

What do you think happens next?

He gets his own back by freezing them! Although the clip might make you laugh, here's something that should make nearly all of us **CRY!**

I believe if **99%** of salon owners in the UK had to go on the programme to make a pitch to get funding for their salon, they would get a **'frosty'** response as well!

I know it's a harsh point I'm making but as a **'business'** many salons are a bit of a 'joke'. So what would change that? What sort of business case would a salon have to create to become attractive to a Dragon?

I think the Dragons would be looking for 3 things.

1. They'd be looking for an idea, product or concept with a clearly defined target market.
2. They'd be looking to see that the people behind the business are committed, passionate and able.
3. They'd be looking for the business to give them a significant return on their investment.

How do you think your 'business' would measure up to what they're looking for? Let's find out.

Ask yourself:

- Could I tell them about my clearly defined target market?
- Could I tell them about the Unique Perceived Benefit my salon offers

my clients? *(The UPB might be a new concept for you; if it is, don't worry I explain it in detail in the next chapter.)*
- Could I prove to them I'm committed and passionate about creating a successful 'business'?
- Could I convince them I've got the ability to do it?
- Could I prove to them they'd get a good financial return on their investment?

If the answer to any of these questions is no and you're determined your salon is going to be more than just a 'job' you can now see more clearly what you need to improve.

We're going to look at **'Marketing'** in the next chapter and we've already looked at the need to build your belief in yourself; so in this chapter we're going to focus on the area most salon owners have the biggest problem with, which is their **'Financials'** and the key to mastering those is:

MEASUREMENT!

Measurement; it's not the most exciting word in the dictionary, is it! But when we understand its power and look at it in the right way it can become very motivating.

After all, how much fun would a game of football be if you didn't know what the score was? How much fun would 'Who wants to be a millionaire?' be if we didn't know the value of the questions the contestants were answering?

You need to see measuring your business as **'motivating'**. So have fun and set yourself some measurable targets and get really excited when you achieve them. Do the same for your team and share their results with them in a positive exciting way.

Why is it an expensive mistake not to think like a **'Dragon'** and measure everything?

It's because it costs you money to open a salon. I'm sure you'll agree that it's not unusual for Salon Owners to invest more than £50,000 on this.

You need to get that money back quickly, preferably in the first **2** or **3** years, so you've got time to save for your first re-fit. If you're not measuring your profit, you won't know how you're doing.

It costs you money to run a salon and we need to remember there are only **100 pence** in every pound. No matter how much we wish there could be more! Think of every pound like a cake with 100 slices.

By the way, if you're not based in the UK and your currency is Dollars or Euros instead, you've got the same 100 slice cake, just with different coloured icing on top! The point I'm making is the principles are **exactly** the same; just remember there are only 100 cents to the Euro and the Dollar as well: **and you're in business to make a profit!**

Anyway, here in the UK if you're VAT registered the Government will take 12 slices of your cake or 12p out of every pound before you start, leaving you with 88 left. *(In case you're wondering why it's not 17.5 slices it's because the government allow you to claim about 5.5 slices back, leaving you with 12.)*

Then you need to put 20 slices of your cake or 20p out of every pound to one side for yourself as net profit. This is something most salon owners don't do, they don't **plan** to make a profit, they just cross their fingers, work hard and **'hope'!**

Are you guilty of that?

Building your profit into your calculations is vital for at least 6 reasons.

Profit:

1. Pays you back your initial investment;
2. Rewards you for taking the risk, because running a business is always a risk; *just think how easy it is to go bust, get sued or be taken to a tribunal;*
3. Gives you money to invest in the future;

4. Allows you to expand the business;
5. Enables you to acquire assets;
6. Builds a pension fund to provide for your retirement and so on.

If you've been counting, you'll know that once VAT and your profit have been put to one side you've got 68 slices of cake or 68 pence in each pound left to pay for **everything** else; which is not a lot is it!

I find budgeting helps here.

Every three months I estimate what I think my turnover will be and then I work out how much I can afford to spend on wages, stock and everything else. At the end of the 3 months I look at my accounts and see if it all worked out as planned.

In my ***"SOS"*** *system* I have a Quarterly Budget Sheet that helps me do this and as always you can download a copy for yourself from the website. By the way, I recommend **very** strongly that you have a set of profit and loss accounts done every three months, so you can see in plenty of time if you're spending too much on wages, stock or anything else that's recorded. If, like many salon owners, you only have your accounts done once a year, you're taking a real risk! By the time you know you've got a problem you'll find it's too late to do anything about it: **so don't make that mistake!**

To help you see the whole picture more clearly, here's a brief breakdown of how I plan to spend the 68 pence in the pound that's left after VAT and my profit have been accounted for:

- The biggest expense is staff. *(I budget to spend 40 pence in the pound or less. This includes my own wages and the wages of all my support staff.)*

- The next on the list is stock. *(I budget to spend 15 pence in the pound or less.)*

- Rent and rates. *(I budget to spend 5 pence in the pound or less.)*

- Finally, everything else: Marketing, training, heat and light, telephone, refreshments and so on. *(If you've been doing your sums you'll know there are only **8** pence in the pound left to pay for all these, so spend your money wisely!)*

In case you're wondering, here's an easy way to work out your percentages using a calculator. Take wages, for example. You'll need your wages cost for the quarter and your VAT inclusive turnover for the **same** period.

Now; enter your wages cost into the calculator and press the ÷ symbol; next enter your total turnover figure and press the % symbol and there's your answer!

So for example; if your wages were £87,000 and your turnover was £153,000 your calculation would look like this.

87,000 ÷ 153,000 then press the % key = 57%

As we mentioned your wages bill is your biggest expense so your staff performance needs to be measured constantly. The easiest way to do it is with a Point Of Sale computer system which measures the performance of your whole business. I couldn't imagine running a salon without one. Any time I want to check anything it only takes a couple of minutes - **brilliant!**

Over the years I've used 5 different systems and I have to say I like the one I use now the best. Why do I like it? Because it's good value for money, the training and support is excellent and as well as measuring everything, it's also a fantastic marketing tool.

The system is called **Phorest** and if you're interested you can find out more by going to the link on the website.

Anyway, let's get back to your wages bill. The key thing you have to measure is your stylists' cost, relative to their takings. Their wages, *including commission*, should be no more than 30% to 32% of their turnover all the time **not just on the odd busy day or week.**

Why is this **THE MOST IMPORTANT** thing you can measure?

Because an out of control wages bill is the single biggest **'expensive mistake'** I see salon owners making, and far too many have no idea which stylists are giving them value for money and which stylists are crippling their business.

To guard against this problem I set my stylists the target of taking at least 4 times their basic wage each week.

I provide commission and incentives to take them beyond this level but they get a yellow card, then a red card if they fall below it for long. *By the way, if a stylist is recently qualified I give them a year to start hitting that target. If they join me from another salon with no clients they get 6 months to start hitting it. If they join me from another salon with clients they get 3 months.*

I could write a complete book on the financial aspects of running a salon but for now just remember being **'busy'** isn't the same as making a **profit**, an important lesson that can be summed up with this mantra:

Turnover is Vanity ... Profit is sanity!

Remember, you can see the 'Dragons Den' clip, find the Phorest link, and download the ***"SOS"*** *system* quarterly budget sheet at **www.7expensivemistakes.com**

"What I've learned has saved me and my business."

"I love the fact that Simon tells it how it is! In this no fuss, no nonsense, book he talks about the trials salon owners face on a daily basis. With his wealth of knowledge he helps us focus on and work through many of the challenges that face us.

Quite simply what I've learned has saved me and my business."

Stephen McCartney, The Cutting Room

Expensive Mistake Number 6
Giving the 'GOSSIPS' the chance to ruin your business!

As I mentioned a few pages ago, in this chapter we're going to look at marketing ... **but what is marketing?**

As salon owners, we all know we **need** to do it, but most of us don't truly understand what it is and how to do it cost effectively.

Many of us think it's about special offers, promotions and advertising; and it is, **partly!**

But it's also more, **a lot more**.

It's about:

- Everything that makes our salons interesting to potential clients;
- Anything that gets us noticed and talked about;
- Anything that makes us exciting, attractive or worthy of comment;
- Anything that creates **'word of mouth'**, or **'word of media'** interest.

I wonder what people say about **your** salon?

What do you give them to talk about?

I hope its lots of:

- Positive news;
- Great offers;
- Professional advice;
- Education.

I hope it's not about:

- The state of your toilets;
- The stains on your towels;

- The fact that your staff don't seem to care, because they're too busy gossiping or falling out with each other to pay much attention to any one else!

I hope it's not about the time:

- You kept them waiting;
- Overcharged them;
- Your drains smelled awful;
- Your new receptionist ignored them while she chatted on the phone to a friend!

Give them half a chance and most clients are more than happy to revel in gossiping and moaning about the bad stuff that happens, no matter how **good** your haircuts are!

OUCH!

We must never forget there's always someone waiting to re-interpret anything that happens in your salon to make it more gossip worthy, just like on **"Have I Got News for You'** a long running TV program which is now in its **38th** series. In the clip I've selected there is much mirth and fun being extracted from the celebrations to mark the 20th anniversary of the fall of the Berlin Wall.

Don't forget, if you want to watch it, you can see the clip on the 7 Expensive Mistakes website.

You'll see them take a celebration of one of the most important events of the last century and simply by talking about it from a humorous point of view, distort it into something quite different.

So the question I want you to think about is **how can you take control of the 'News' agenda of your salon?**

If you don't, **others** will do it for you.

The first thing to work on is making sure your salon is clean, tidy, well organised and that it runs to time. You must understand that this is a very important part of your marketing message.

Next you need to make sure you've got a great atmosphere. How do you make sure the atmosphere's great? By realising you live in a world that's become very detached and impersonal. This knowledge gives you the perfect opportunity to stand out from the crowd and make clients feel important and cared for.

Here are some tips to help you and your staff to deliver a great salon atmosphere:

- **Smile genuinely.** When you make eye contact with every client and smile, you'll see them smile back.

- **Give sincere compliments.** Stop focussing on yourself and pay every client two or three sincere compliments. It shows you care.

- **Use your client's name.** Remember, the sweetest sound is someone's own name. Find out what they like to be called and try using it 4 or 5 times during an appointment.

- **Make regular eye contact.** Make sure you look directly into your client's eyes when they talk to you. This will show them you're interested.

- **Use humour.** It's OK to be playful and get silly sometimes. Don't be afraid to laugh, it's infectious.

- **Never argue with a client.** You can never **ever** win in the long run, even if a client is wrong! Remember this isn't a game and we're not fighting a war either, we're running a business.

- **If there's a problem, keep calm.** Don't get dragged into the drama or emotional tension a problem can create.

- **Fix the experience.** Remember, if a client is unhappy it's not enough to fix the problem, you have to fix the **experience**. It's how they feel afterwards that matters.

Please don't ignore these tips. They may be simple but they are priceless.

If you make the mistake of taking your clients for granted you'll regret it in the end. As I said earlier you have to focus on getting the basic experience right first. Then and **only** then, when you're sure you can really deliver on the promises you make, is it safe to start on what most people think of as marketing.

Spending money on advertising and promotions when the basic experience you're offering isn't right **is a very expensive mistake**. It means you're spending money attracting people to your business just to show them you've got problems!

Very clever ... **NOT!**

But let's assume you've got the basics right, what comes next? A salon newsletter would be a great place to start. Combine it with a lively, fun, interactive website and a membership club with special perks for your clients and you'll be well set.

If you're not sure what to say in your newsletter or on your site, you need to learn how to make things 'newsworthy'. Have a look in some newspapers, magazines, or on the web and you'll see what the professionals do to grab your attention.

They focus on things that are:

- The first;
- The latest;
- The oldest;
- The biggest;
- The smallest;

- New;
- Improved;
- An anniversary celebration;
- Award winning;

I could go on!

To create news you can also:

- Give your opinion on something that's making the news. *For example as I write this Cheryl Cole is in the news for promoting a L'Oreal shampoo that strengthens her hair and gives it volume and bounce ... when in fact she wearing extensions! You could comment on that couldn't you!*
- Give something away **FREE**. *(More on this later!)*
- Hold a survey, or comment on the results of a survey.
- Support a charity.
- Solve a problem for your clients.
- Attempt to beat or set a record.
- Create a publicity stunt based on characters in a hit film.

And so on, and so on.

By the way, half the battle in making something newsworthy is creating a great headline, because the headline is the **'marketing'** for the **'marketing'**! If it doesn't attract your attention, it doesn't matter how good the rest of the message is, it won't be read.

Here's a great tip that will help you create a never ending stream of fantastic headlines:

- Grab some copies of the popular magazines that are bound to be available in your salon.
- Next, write a list of all the headlines you see on the front covers on a piece of paper.
- Then you can go down the list and adapt the best ones to fit whatever it is you're talking about!

To show you how easy this is to do, I've just picked up a copy of **Good Housekeeping**. Here's a list of the headlines on the front cover:

- 10 Feel good ways to afford the life you want!
- What's normal and what's not? The no panic guide to your health.
- Transform yourself ... "We changed our looks and our lives."
- Get more energy naturally and protect your immunity too.

Let's play with these and see how you could adapt them for use in your salon newsletter or on your website.

How about:

- 10 Feel good styles you can afford to wear!
- What's normal and what's not? The no panic guide to unexpected hair loss!
- Transform your hair ... transform your life!
- Give your hair more energy and bounce by following these 7 simple tips!

Do you see what I mean? It's an easy way of coming up with attention grabbing headlines and an easy way to get ideas for interesting articles you can write as well. Now if I can do this with headlines from a magazine that's as mundane as **Good Housekeeping** what could you do with the headlines from something far punchier like **Cosmo!!!**

Here's another tip that will help you make your marketing more 'newsworthy'. Collect testimonials and stories of positive experiences from your clients and use them wherever you can in your marketing.

Why are testimonials and client stories such a good idea? Simply because if **you** say something ... in the back of your clients mind you're selling, no matter how nicely you do it. But if another client says something or if it's a story about another clients experience, its interesting **NEWS!**

Here are some simple tips to help you collect them:

- Interview your clients. You'll find a simple interview sheet from my

***"SOS"** system* that will help you do this on the website.

- Send or give out a **'Testimonials by the dozen'** letter to your clients and watch them pour in. Again you'll find a letter from my ***"SOS"** sys tem* you can use for doing this on the website.

- Set up a client testimonial/feedback voicemail line. You can do this for FREE! You'll find a link to a company who will give you **2** dedicated voicemail numbers and send you the recordings clients leave as email attachments, for FREE on the website.

Once your line is set up, just promote the voicemail number, which you can do by putting a tag paragraph on the end of articles in your newsletter and on your website. In your tag paragraph, tell them the story they've just been reading was left on your **'dedicated client feedback line'** then you can add, how much you love hearing about their experiences, opinions and stories. Tell them how easy it is for them to do the same, all they have to do is call and leave a message. ***You could even give a reward for every message that's used or left.***

Remember, if there's always something new, different or exciting going on it will give your clients positive things to talk about, ***which has got to be good news!***

But there's more to marketing than just making sure what you do is newsworthy. Here are 6 secrets that will help you do a really great job with your marketing.

Secret Number 1.

Create a comprehensive salon database.

As an absolute minimum you must have on record, the first name, surname, address, mobile phone number and e mail address of **EVERY CLIENT** who comes into your salon.

Any hairdressing business that doesn't have an accurate, up to date client database is throwing away money. Here are 3 very good reasons why you should do it.

Reason 1.

You can use appointment reminders to save you money and put a stop to no shows.

Today it's easy to do these by text or email if you have a computerised appointment book like the one you'll find on the 'Phorest' system I've recommended.

The good thing about appointment reminders is they show your clients you're professional, you care and you take your time seriously. If **you** take your time seriously your clients are more likely to do it as well, aren't they? Also you'll be pleased to know, nearly every salon that introduces reminder texts see a dramatic reduction in the number of clients who forget to turn up!

Reason 2.

You can use ***'we've missed you letters'*** to bring back some of the clients you've 'lost'.

Research has shown you lose clients for one of 4 reasons:

1. They died.
2. They moved away
3. You did something wrong, either a technical mistake or you took them for granted.
4. Something in their life interrupted them and they got out of the habit.

You can't do anything about reasons 1 and 2 but you certainly can with numbers 3 and 4.

- The first step is to be aware it's happening and your salon computer system will tell you, if you look.

- The second step is to get in contact and genuinely ask them if they're alright.

By the way if you're going to contact them, research has shown that a personalised **"we've missed you"** letter is much better than the mass produced 'come back' leaflet or voucher many salons use.

Try following these simple steps when writing your letter:

- Tell them you've noticed they don't come in any more.
- Say you hope they're alright and that you're concerned about them.
- Tell them in a caring way that you want to make sure that you didn't do anything wrong.
- Tell them if you or your team **did** do something wrong, you'll be happy to do whatever it takes to make it right again.
- Finally, make them an offer they can't refuse.

What I've found since we've been using letters like this in my salon is that reason number 4, something in their life interrupted them and they got out of the habit, is the most common. The fact that we've cared enough to write is enough to bring them back. Remember, every client you **'save'** is like winning a new client, so once you get them back don't take them for granted.

Reason 3.

You can say **'Thank You'** which makes clients feel special.

One of the best times to start saying thank you to a client is a few days after their first appointment. Did you know that new clients are **8** times more likely to become regular clients if they get past their **3rd** appointment?

To me, that information suggests a thank you letter to encourage them would be a good idea **wouldn't it!** But it's only the beginning. There are many great ways to say **'thank you'** to clients. Why not see how many others you and your team can come up with.

So, now you know how important it is to have every client's details on record, what's the best way to collect them?

It's simple ... set up a membership program. We call it the **VIP client program** in my salon. We give every client who joins a £15 voucher to spend in the salon ***but only if they complete the application form.***

Guess what information we ask for.

That's right:

- First Name;
- Surname;
- Mobile number;
- E Mail Address;
- Home Address;
- Home Phone number;

Now we can:

- Remind them about their next appointment.
- Send them their 'recommend a friend' rewards.
- Send them their monthly newsletter.
- Invite them to the VIP Client Evenings.
- Let them know about the next VIP pamper days.
- Tell them about the special offers we've arranged for them from other local businesses.

Can you see why clients are happy to give us their details! Can you see why a client database gives you the ability to take control of your business?

Secret Number 2.

Communicate with your clients regularly.

Why?

It's because we're in a competitive industry. Do you realise that every day your competitors are trying to steal **your** clients? Only this morning I was talking to a salon owner who was very upset because one of her competitors was spreading rumours that she was closing!

What can you do to tackle problems like this? The only thing that really works in the long run is making sure your clients know you care. What makes the difference between a client who knows you care and one who doesn't?

Regular communication!

You already have a relationship with your existing clients, and your competitors don't, **YET**, so you have the advantage!

Your job is to deny them the chance to take your advantage away from you by continually strengthening and building the relationship.

> **Fact: It's a mistake to leave this to your staff because being fallible human beings, they <u>won't</u> do it consistently.**

You have to communicate regularly and consistently and we've already talked about lots of tools you can use to do it with, haven't we. Just remember that whatever you communicate has to be valuable to your clients. It needs to be newsworthy and either educate them or make them an offer that shows you care. You need to make sure you focus on what's in it for them ***because that's what they're interested in.***

This means for example, if you've got a new product to talk about:

- Tell them about the problem it solves.
- Tell them about the money they'll save.
- Tell them about how it's going to make them feel.
- Tell them about the results other people have been getting with it.
- Tell them about the guarantee you're offering with it.
- Make them an offer they can't refuse!

That's what they want to hear from you.

Secret Number 3.

Understand Your 'Unique Perceived Benefit'

This is not a phrase most of us have heard of so you're probably wondering what I'm talking about, but it's simple really.

Your **'Unique Perceived Benefit' (UPB)** is a statement you use to make your salon stand out from the crowd, so it will be seen as **DIFFERENT** from your competitors. Don't you think it would be great if your salon 'stood out from the crowd'?

Of course it would!!

Now occasionally, when you look at what you do, you'll find your UPB is obvious, but in most cases you need to **'create'** it from scratch and I'll show you how in a moment.

Once you've done it though:

- Your UPB becomes your catchphrase or motto.
- It becomes the thing you're **'known'** for.
- Your job is to spread your UPB message clearly and consistently in a way your marketplace can't ignore.

I can't stress enough how important this is to you.

How can you expect people to choose you, over and above any other salon, if they can't quickly see what it is you do that's so right for them?

I promised to show you how to create your UPB and the easiest way to do it, is show you the most successful one there's ever been ... ***so here it is!***

Fresh Hot Pizza Delivered To Your Door In 30 Minutes Or Less, or It's Free ... Domino's Pizza

Tom Monahan of Domino's Pizza created one of the most successful fast-food franchises in the world using this UPB.

What makes it so good? Well, for a start, just notice that Tom doesn't say he sells 'the best tasting pizza'. It wouldn't work because it's a matter of opinion; just like you saying *"we do the best haircuts"* wouldn't work, because it's only your opinion!

What he does do though, is promise his customers exactly what they really want and gives them a guarantee they'll get it.

They want it hot, they want it quickly and he guarantees to deliver in 30 minutes 'or it's FREE'.

That's what your UPB needs to do, promise a result to your clients and guarantee they'll get it! So what result could you promise?

Well, promises based on clients saving time, saving money, or getting something extra for nothing usually work the best. Why not have a brain storming session with your staff and see what you can come up with.

How would you guarantee it?

That's up to you and how confident you are of delivering, but I'll tell you this, having a guarantee is a real benefit to you because it:

- Raises your standards and gives you a reputation to live up to.
- Gives you valuable feedback about problems, because more clients will **bother** to tell you if they're not happy: *At the moment most unhappy clients just go home and tell everyone else, which is not what you want!*
- Encourages far more **'new'** clients to come in and try you because your guarantee will give them confidence.

So get past the thing that worries most salon owners when I suggest they use a guarantee, which is they're afraid clients will rip them off. All the research shows very few actually do. If you've got the guts to offer one you'll get a better salon **and** lots of new clients.

There's another great reason why you musn't be seen as the same as other salons. **What is it?** Well, if you're not seen as different, what do you think becomes the most important factor people base their choice on?

That's right: **price!**

Your **UPB** takes you out of the **'price war'** because you're no longer seen as the **<u>same</u>** as other salons!

Now, I like to practice what I preach, so later in the book you'll find another good example of a UPB in action. Keep your eyes open and see if you can spot it!

<u>Secret Number 4.</u>

Find out what you're up against by mystery shopping your competitors' salons ... and your own as well!

It pays to be aware of the standards your competitors are setting, and mystery shopping is a great way to find out. It's simple to set up a program. Get together a small group of people who love having their hair done and are capable of writing a report afterwards.

Brief them on what you're looking for and give them a questionnaire to fill in after their visit. If it helps you'll find a readymade mystery shopper questionnaire from my ***"SOS"*** *system* on the 7 Expensive Mistakes website.

Get them to make and keep an appointment and then give them 2 days **<u>max</u>** to fill in the form. Then you can sit down with them, go over their notes and see what you've learned.

It's all common sense isn't it? And taking the time to do this will confirm what you're doing well and open your eyes to possible opportunities you might be missing.

By the way, I meant what I said about mystery shopping your own salon as well.

Another pair of eyes looking at what's going on won't do any harm! Research has shown that the quality of hairdressing you offer is surprisingly low on a client's list of priorities. They're likely to be more concerned about feeling comfortable, how clean and well organised your salon is and whether you keep them waiting.

Mystery shopping will give you a lot of valuable information about all these things.

Secret Number 5.

Tap into the power of direct response marketing.

Direct response marketing is exactly what the name suggests; its marketing you **know** clients have **'responded'** to. Here's an example to help you see what I mean.

If you were to put an advert in the paper that says:

Curl Up and Dye.

- **Unisex Hair Salon**
- **Open 7 days.**
- **Appointments not needed.**
- **Prices start at £10**

It would be an image ad. You can see it just gives a list of facts and features about the salon. ***It might work for you, but there's no way you'd ever know for sure, is there.***

If however, your advert said:

Curl Up and Dye.

- **Unisex Hair Salon**
- **Open 7 days.**
- **Bring this advert in before 01/01/01 and we'll give you a Special Gift Voucher for £5**
- **Appointments not needed.**
- **Prices start at £10**

You'd be able to find out. All you'd have to do is count up the number of **£5** gift vouchers you issued to discover how many people responded, wouldn't you. Then it's easy to work out if the advert paid for itself or not.

If it did, you'd be mad not to run it again next week. Try it with a different headline and see if more people claim a **£5** voucher or not. If more people come in, ***stick with the new headline and change something else about the ad.***

See if that works better or not. By a process of testing and elimination you'll end up with brilliant adverts that are guaranteed to make you money.

Here are some important rules for testing your adverts:

- Start this process with small inexpensive ads while you're going through the testing process.
- Only when you have a small advert that's proved it can pay for itself does it make sense to **GO LARGE.**
- When you do you'll find the response will increase dramatically.
- When you're testing, make sure you only change one thing at a time on your advert; ***otherwise you won't know which change made your ad perform better or worse.***

These principles can be used in all types of marketing, not just adverts. Just remember ... don't spend a penny on marketing unless you can measure the results. Tesco's, L'Oreal and Coca Cola can afford image advertising, **you can't!**

Secret Number 6.
Tap into the power of 'FREE'.

We mentioned **'FREE'** earlier but let's just spell it out for you in more detail. When you give your clients the 'little extras' and 'nice touches' you add a great deal of **'emotion'** to your relationship and it can make a big difference.

In my salon we give clients:

- A rose at valentines.
- An Easter Egg at Easter time.
- A Birthday card with a **£10** voucher.
- A Christmas card with a thank you letter and some vouchers to keep us busy in January and February.

What little gifts could you give your clients throughout the year?

You can also add power to your marketing with offers that are based on the word 'free'. It's not only new clients who respond to free. You can modify or re-enforce your existing clients behaviour by giving give them free stuff, if they do what you want.

For example:

- Make your next appointment as you leave, and when you keep it we'll give you a **free** bottle of shampoo.
- For every **£10** you spend we'll give you 1 point. When you've got **5** points we'll give you a **free** blow dry.
- Next time you come to the salon bring a friend who's not been before, and we'll do their hair for **free** as a gift from you.

The permutations are endless but never underestimate the power of **free.** Research has shown it's the most effective word you can use in your marketing and relationship building efforts.

OK, we've covered a lot of different marketing ideas in this chapter, haven't we? But here's one last thought.

Do your marketing well and it's easy to find you've become **20%** more successful at:

1. *Attracting new clients;*
2. *Getting existing clients to spend more;*
3. *Getting existing clients to come in more frequently;*
4. *Keeping existing clients loyal to you for longer.*

If you do become 20% more successful **all** those things you'll find your turnover has more than doubled! Let's go through the sums and prove it.

We want to make it easy to calculate so imagine your salon has:

- **1000** clients who spend
- **£20** per visit and come in
- **5** times per year and stay loyal for
- **1** year

Your sum looks like this:

1000 clients X **£20 spend** X **5** visits = **£100,000 turnover**

Now let's improve all those figures by **'only' 20%**

- **1000** clients + 20% becomes **1200**
- **£20** +20% becomes **£24**
- **5** visits + 20% becomes **6** visits
- **1** years loyalty + 20% becomes **14.4** months; which means the total number of visits your average client makes goes up from **5** to **7**

So your new sum looks like this:

1200 clients X £24 spend X 7 visits = £201,600 turnover

An improvement of **101.6%**

And that's not all; the value of each new client you attracted has gone up as well! Look at the figures and you'll see.

Before we improved everything by just **20%** an **'average'** client came in **5** times and spent **£20** making them worth **£100**

After we improved everything by just **20%** ... an average client comes in **7** times and spends **£24** making them worth **£168**

So by making a small improvement in several areas, every new client is suddenly worth **68% more**:

WOW!

Now do you see why marketing isn't an optional extra we can afford to leave to the gossip mongers and **'Have I got News for you'** word of mouth brigade!

Now do you see why it's a **MASSIVE** mistake to simply focus on attracting new clients when you should also spend just as much time growing the business you get from existing clients by working on their:

- *Frequency of visit;*
- *Average spend;*
- *Loyalty!*

Remember, you can see the 'Have I got News for you' clip and download my ***"SOS"*** *system*: interview sheet, 'Testimonials by the dozen' letter and 'Mystery Client' questionnaire from **www.7expensivemistakes.com**

"It's easy to read, easy to understand and easy to implement."

"I first met Simon after a talk he gave to a number of salon owners. I sat in that room listening to a man describing all my business problems ... and he gave me hope.

Up to that point I'd felt very alone in my salon with all the problems I couldn't solve. I learned that day that I wasn't alone. I'm now using, on a daily basis, the advice Simon has put in this book and frankly, the difference between my "old" and "new" life is like night and day.

The stresses and strains of not understanding myself, my staff or how a business really works have now been reduced to the odd, easily solved, hiccup. No more going home to my family in the evenings a total emotional wreck ... so it's made my home life better too!

Imagine having a toolkit where you have just the right tool to sort the job, well ... this book is it! What's more, it's easy to read, easy to understand and easy to implement.

I will guarantee if you use his advice, use the tools and go to work ON your business, you WILL fix it.

I Did!"

Billy Mann, The Good Hair Company

Expensive Mistake Number 7
Missing 'The X Factor'!

Can you remember meeting someone special for the first time and thinking WOW, nice looks, great body, and warm smile; you ***really were <u>attracted</u> to this person.***

But when you've got to know them better, you find their annoying habits and different values start to emerge. You discover they're not the person you thought they were ***and you're left looking for a way out of the relationship!***

In the beginning they had 'The **'X factor',** that indefinable **'something'** that attracted you, ***but it didn't last!***

At the time of writing this book the **X Factor 2009** series has just finished on TV and something similar happened there. If you're addicted to the programme like I am, you'll have seen the auditions. If you watch them again now with the benefit of hindsight, you can tell from the expressions on the judges faces and the reaction of the audience **Danyl Johnson** had more of the **'X' Factor** than **Joe Mc Elderry,** the eventual winner

If you want to check for yourself, you can see clips of both Danyl and Joe's auditions on the 7 Expensive Mistakes website.

So what happened?

Because of his impact at the auditions, Danyl's support from the public started off strongly and he won the public vote 3 times in the early rounds, then as time went by the negative publicity he generated had an effect and his support dropped away.

On the other hand it took Joe six weeks before he came top of the public vote, but from then on he won every time. We need our salons to be like Joe; we want everyone to be attracted to it and we want that attraction to grow *not fade away because of negative gossip and publicity like it did for Danyl.*

When I say we want 'everyone' to be attracted to your salon; I mean by everyone; you, your staff and your clients. To understand how we make it happen for 'everyone' we need answers to these questions:

- What would make a salon owner want to keep a business for a life time?
- What would make staff want to work there for their whole career?
- What would make clients want to stay loyal to a salon and rave about it to their friends?

They're good questions, so let's dig a bit deeper. Would you feel your salon has the **'X factor'** if you were:

- Making lots of money?
- Working for as much or little time as you want?
- Working with a team of people who you respect and trust because they're low maintenance and work hard?
- Only doing the things you find 'fun' and 'enjoyable' because everything else was being done for you?
- Recognised within the industry as being a success?

Do you think your staff would feel your salon has the **'X factor'** if they were:

- Well paid?
- Well trained?
- Trusted and appreciated?
- Treated fairly?
- Given responsibility?
- Encouraged to aspire to and attain career goals?

Do you think your clients would feel your salon has the **'X factor'** if it was:

- A place where they feel important?
- Managed by people who understand what they want and deliver it consistently?
- Comfortable, friendly and easy to belong to?
- Staffed by people they like and respect?

- A place where they get value for money?

A salon that could deliver all that, to all those **different** people, would be a pretty special place wouldn't it? It would certainly be a salon that everyone would have an emotional bond with. It would have that indefinable something that would attract people and keep them loyal. I think by any standard of measurement it would have **'The X Factor'.**

By the way, I want you to notice I've put the 3 groups we've just talked about in a very specific order.

1. The owner first;
2. Then the staff;
3. Finally the clients.

Let me ask ***"Does this seem back to front to you?"***

I wondered, because I often ask salon owners this question, and **99%** of the time they tell me I've got it wrong ***they think the clients should come first on the list.***

Let me explain why I believe that's an expensive mistake and why it would pay you to look at it the other way round. A salon doesn't just **happen**. Someone has to have the idea, get the money together and take the risk. That someone is the owner.

No owner = no salon = no jobs = no clients.

See what I mean? It all starts with the owner; a salon **'has'** to meet the needs of the owner first. If it doesn't, ***in the long run the business will either be sold or die a long lingering death!***

Do you need more proof that the owner's feelings are the most important? Well, try looking at it this way.

If an owner isn't X factor happy:

- They won't be an X factor boss;

- They won't attract X factor staff;
- Clients won't get X factor service!

So for staff and clients to be X factor happy in the long run, the owner has to be X factor happy first.

Put another way.

X factor clients can only be looked after by X factor staff and
X factor staff will only work for an X factor boss.

It all comes back to you and making sure you get the X factor first. You'll then make sure your staff get it. They'll then make damn sure they give X factor service to their clients because it's the best way of keeping their X factor job with an X factor boss.

The X factor starts and ends with you!

There's a reason why we've tackled the X factor **'expensive mistake'** last, and it's because most of the tools you need to use to give your salon **'The X Factor'** have already been given to you as we've learned about the previous 6 mistakes. We needed to understand them first before we could add this last piece to the jigsaw.

So let's remind ourselves of what we've already covered, then we can add the missing piece although I've already given you a BIG hint as to what it is.

An X factor boss:

- Has a positive self image.

- Sticks to their 'strengths' and delegates round their weaknesses.

- Only employs people with the right attitude, values and behaviour, doesn't try to please or placate the 'Hyacinths' but politely and with respect ***moves them on***.

- Knows how to avoid the **'Golden Balls'** trap because continually em ploying the wrong people, only to discover the mistake later, is ***time consuming, expensive and gets in the way of growth.***

- Has a salon that makes sense as a **'business'**, with effective systems in place to **'measure'** the key performance indicators, so they know if it's performing well ***whether they are there or not.***

- Has an effective **'marketing system'** in place, so the business is con tinually spreading a positive news agenda that attracts new clients and rewards existing clients.

That's a brief summary of what we've covered so far, isn't it? ***So what's missing?***

What's been implied and suggested, but not spelt out? What's the glue that holds everything together? I'll tell you. ***"The missing ingredient is found in the principles of EQ."***

Not sure what EQ is?

It's the measurement of 'Emotional Intelligence' which is our ability to understand and communicate with the emotions of other people. People who are intelligent have a high IQ; people who are emotionally intelligent have a high EQ.

If your business is designed to meet the emotional needs of you, your staff and your clients, **then it will really have the X factor!**

Why is it so important?

Because all the research shows that emotions drive human behaviour, ***NOT LOGIC.***

Go back to the list of things that **'X factor'** bosses, staff and clients want and you'll see it's littered with emotion words such as:

- **Like**
- **Trust**
- **Respect**
- **Appreciate**

The good news is that while your IQ score stays much the same throughout your life, your EQ score can rise dramatically if you do the right things! What are the right things? Just about everything I've shared with you in this book, ***that's what makes it so <u>powerful</u>!***

You'll find your EQ will grow when you:

- Feel good about who you are and what you want.
- Focus on what you're good at.
- Surround yourself with people who you trust and can work with.
- Organise your business properly.
- Communicate clearly and positively with everyone.

Fact: It will pay you more than you can <u>ever</u> imagine to develop a high EQ for yourself, *because a high EQ business will follow, like night follows day.*

Your high EQ business will have '**The X Factor**' and you'll get:

- The staff;
- The clients;
- The salon;
- The life;

you've always wanted ***and will definitely deserve.***

If you want to understand more, much more, about developing your EQ I'd recommend a book called: **Primal Leadership**; ***realising the power of emotional intelligence*** by Daniel Goleman.

You won't be surprised to know by now you can see the X factor clips and find a link to more information about Primal Leadership at **<u>www.7expensivemistakes.com</u>**

Finally
What's next for you?

Believe me when I say, if you make a commitment to start reversing the damage the **'7 most expensive mistakes'** are doing to your business, it will have a '**huge**' effect on your performance; and will lead you to a highly profitable, fulfilling salon, more rapidly than you **ever** expected.

But there's a question you need to ask: "**Do you have the time and skills to do it on your own?**"

If your answer is **'yes'** then great. You've got the book as a guide. You've got the resources I've provided on the 7 Expensive Mistakes website to support you. All you need to add is ***Action!***

Nothing happens without it and I wish you every success.

On the other hand, if you feel you don't have the time to put everything together, or you can't see how you're going to get started, you might want to take a closer look at my ***"SOS"*** *system.*

When you do, you'll see it's been designed to take the pressure off **you**; *once that happens you'll find your salon starts working better very quickly.*

If you take advantage of my ***"SOS"*** *system* you'll soon have a salon that's working properly because all your:

- *Marketing;*
- *Health and safety;*
- *Staff recruitment;*
- *Staff training;*
- *Staff motivation;*
- *Artistic leadership;*
- *Customer service and;*
- *Strategic planning responsibilities;*

will be organised for you because my team and I will work with you to apply the ***"SOS"*** *system* right through your business. This will have a '**huge**' effect on your performance and how you feel about your salon.

The really good news is you can try my ***"SOS"*** *system* and the support you get with it FREE for a month, with no obligation and if you decide to continue, it's **guaranteed** to pay for itself in increased profits ... or it's **FREE!**

If you've been paying attention, *and I'm sure you have*, you'll have noticed I've just given you the great example of a UPB in action I promised you earlier! I've just made you an offer and given you a guarantee ... haven't I!

If you feel my offer and the guarantee look like something you want to know more about, either call us on 01205 366599 and we'll send you an information pack or go to the 'What's next' page at **www.7expensivemistakes.com** and download one ... but don't think about it for too long, because places on the support system are limited and you might have to wait longer than you really want to for a slot!

Here's a final thought I want to leave you with.

You now know all about **the 7 most expensive mistakes salon owners make**; your future is in front of you; you have a choice ... and its **decision** time.

Are you going to be the salon owner who reads a book like this, makes a vague promise to take action and then does ... **absolutely nothing!**

Or are you going to step up to the mark and decide to:

- Take control of your self image;
- Take control of your salon;
- Take control of your life;
- Climb out of your 'RUT' and step confidently into your **'X factor'** future!

I hope so because:

**"If you keep on doing what you've always done...
You'll keep on getting what you've always got!"**

Is that what you really want?